Practicing
Affirmation

Practicing
Affirmation

*God-Centered Praise
of Those Who Are Not God*

SAM CRABTREE

Foreword by John Piper

WHEATON, ILLINOIS

Practicing Affirmation: God-Centered Praise of Those Who Are Not God

Copyright © 2011 by Sam Crabtree

Published by Crossway
                1300 Crescent Street
                Wheaton, Illinois 60187

Interior design and typesetting: Lakeside Design Plus

Cover design: Dual Identity Inc.

First printing 2011

Printed in the United States of America

Trade Paperback ISBN: 978-1-4335-2243-7
PDF ISBN: 978-1-4335-2244-4
Mobipocket ISBN: 978-1-4335-2245-1
ePub ISBN: 978-1-4335-2246-8

Library of Congress Cataloging-in-Publication Data

Crabtree, Sam, 1950–
    Practicing affirmation : God-centered praise of those who are not God / Sam Crabtree.
      p. cm.
    Includes bibliographical references (p.   ) and index.
    ISBN 978-1-4335-2243-7 (tp)
    1. Praise—Religious aspects—Christianity. 2. Interpersonal relations—Religious aspects—Christianity. I. Title.
BV4597.53.P73C73   2011
248.4—dc22   2010044483

Crossway is a publishing ministry of Good News Publishers.

VP		29	28	27	26	25	24	23	22	21	20	19
22	21	20	19	18	17	16	15	14	13	12	11	10

Contents

With thanks to God for those who affirm so well.

Foreword

The point of being created in the image of God is that human beings are destined to display God. That's what images do. And the point of being redeemed by Jesus, and renewed after the image of our Creator, is to recover this destiny.

But why? Surely not so that God's handiwork in his people would go unnoticed or unpraised. If God is sovereign, and every good gift is from above, then not praising the good in others is a kind of sacrilege and soul-sickness.

When our mouths are empty of praise for others, it is probably because our hearts are full of love for self. This is what I mean by soul-sickness. C. S. Lewis was surely right when he wrote,

> The world rings with praise—lovers praising their mistresses, readers their favorite poet, walkers praising the countryside, players praising their favorite game—praise of weather, wines, dishes, actors, motors, horses, colleges, countries, historical personages, children, flowers, mountains, rare stamps, rare beetles, even sometimes politicians or scholars. I had not noticed how the humblest, and at the same time most balanced and capacious,

minds praised most, while the cranks, misfits and malcontents praised least.[1]

Sam's book is a healing balm for cranks, misfits, and malcontents who are so full of self they scarcely see, let alone celebrate, the simple beauties of imperfect virtue in others. Or to say it differently: I need this book.

The absence of affirmation for God's handiwork in his people is also a kind of sacrilege—for at least three reasons.

First, it is disobedience to God's command: "A woman who fears the LORD is to be praised" (Prov. 31:30). And I can't think of any reason why this does not apply in principle to God-fearing men.

Second, it demeans Jesus as though he were stooping to do something unworthy when he says, "Well done, good and faithful servant" (Matt. 25:21, 23). If he says it, should we consider it beneath us to say it?

Third, all the works of God are worthy of praise. And there is no good in anyone but by the work of God (1 Cor. 4:7; 15:10).

It gets deeper. Sam says, "The best affirmation is rooted not only in the character of God, but in the gospel." Which means that every glimmer of good in the life of God's children is blood-bought. Jesus died to make it possible. What does it say about us if he died to bring it about, and we don't consider it worth praising? That is, to say it again, I need this book.

Of course there are pitfalls and problems. What's the difference between good praise and bad flattery? What about the fact that in the Bible God's people never say "Thank you" *to* each other, but only to God *for* each other? What about the danger of encouraging someone's craving for human praise, which Jesus so clearly condemns? Is it okay to want to be on the receiving end of good affirmation? What about unbelievers who are *not* "being renewed after the image of their Creator"? When should

8

we praise them? Or should we not? Sam tackles every one of these issues head on. It is not a superficial book.

But it is practical. Incredibly practical—with dozens of illustrations and applications to the workplace and marriage and parenting and friendships and ministry. And, of course, that's what I would expect from Sam Crabtree. He lives this book. I have worked at Sam's side on the staff of our church since 1997. Which means I have been on the receiving end of unremitting God-focused affirmation. Not without correction. And so, yes, there is a section in the book on that too.

I thank God for you, Sam. I pray that we can finish well together. You have taught me more than you know. You have written a one-of-a-kind book. I have no doubt that in the last day this book will be one of the many reasons the Lord Jesus will say to you, "Well done."

John Piper
Pastor for Preaching and Vision
Bethlehem Baptist Church
Twin Cities, Minnesota

God-Centered Affirmation of Those Who Are Not God

— glorification?

(Affirmation) is the purpose of the universe—specifically, affirmation of God.

Commending the praise of men could meet with justifiable criticism. Landmines are everywhere. Take, for instance, this warning: "The love of our own glory is the greatest competitor with God in our hearts. And sometimes we can cloak this idol in a pious disguise."[1] If this is true, and I think it is, then how can I possibly advocate the praise of people? Am I not fueling idolatrous pride?

The Bible Commends God and People
Even with the Bible's emphasis on humble self-denial and its warnings against pride, the Bible praises people—to the glory

of God, ultimately. The chief end of God is not to glorify man, as humanistic thought would have it; the chief end of man is to glorify God by enjoying him forever. Meanwhile, the praising of people does not necessarily preclude the praising of God, if the people are commended ultimately for his glory. God is glorified in us when we affirm the work he has done and is doing in others.

For example, the Bible commends the majesty of Solomon: "And the LORD made Solomon *very great* in the sight of all Israel and bestowed on him such royal *majesty* as had not been on any king before him in Israel" (1 Chron. 29:25). Note that it is the Lord who made Solomon so great and majestic. Solomon's greatness and majesty are to be recognized and commended, but at the root lay the greatness and majesty of the God who made Solomon so.

The Bible also commends Jabez as being more honorable than his brothers: "Jabez was *more honorable* than his brothers; and his mother called his name Jabez, saying, 'Because I bore him in pain.' Jabez called upon the God of Israel, saying, 'Oh that you would bless me and enlarge my border, and that your hand might be with me, and that you would keep me from harm so that it might not bring me pain!' And God granted what he asked" (1 Chron. 4:9–10). Note that Jabez's honorableness is a result of the grace of the God who grants his requests and enlarges his borders. Jabez, clearly the lesser of the two, makes requests of God, the one who has the power Jabez lacks to fulfill such requests. Jabez's honorableness should be recognized and commended, but it stems from the blessing of God in his life, and the one who is the source of the blessing is the one who deserves the honor for Jabez's honorableness.

The Bible commends the excellent wife of Proverbs 31. It is proper to recognize and commend her excellence. In fact, verse 30 explicitly says, "a woman who fears the LORD is to be praised." Is what? Is to be praised! What I think the Bible is saying there is that a good, proper, healthy, important, and necessary way to praise *people* is to the glory of *God*. In the case of the excellent woman, what is one thing that makes her so excellent? She fears the Lord. God is honored by pointing to the woman's excellence in fearing him, the One who defines and exemplifies excellence.

Isn't Praise of Man Idolatrous?

Praise of man and praise of God can be at odds, but not necessarily. And let me join James in raising the stakes: those who know they should do something—like commend commendable people—but don't do it, are sinning: "So whoever knows the right thing to do and fails to do it, for him it is sin" (James 4:17). So we can sin in two ways: by idolatrous commendation, or by failing to commend the commendable. The challenge for us is to not sin in either direction.

sin of ommission?

When Jesus says, "Render to Caesar the things that are Caesar's, and to God the things that are God's" (Luke 20:25), he is not forbidding that people pay tribute to Caesar. We must be on guard against either/or thinking, when the giving of praise can be both/and. When it is both/and, that is, when we are honoring a person and we are honoring God, it should not look like this:

Honor humans and honor God
(with humans listed first and on an equal plane with God)

Rather, it should look like this:

Honor God
Honor humans
(with God listed first and listed above humans)

affirmation
inspiring

13

commend = praise = encouragement?

By acknowledging that it is God who put the governor in office and by thanking God for the governor when he governs well, we honor both the governor and God, and we honor God more than the governor because we give God the credit for establishing the governor. Also, there may come a day when in love we owe the governor an objection or criticism; we never owe God an objection.

Honoring humans is not necessarily idolatry. Consider the following.

Daniel is not dishonoring God when he praises Nebuchadnezzar, saying "You, O king, the king of kings, to whom the God of heaven has given the kingdom, the power, and the might, and the glory, and into whose hand he has given, wherever they dwell, the children of man, the beasts of the field, and the birds of the heavens, making you rule over them all . . ." (Dan. 2:37–38). The king is glorious, because he has been made so by the God who is more glorious than he. Daniel honors both the king and God by honoring the king in the way he does.

In a later episode, at the first light of dawn when king Darius hurries to the lion's den to see if God had rescued Daniel, Daniel is not diminishing God's honor by saying to king Darius, "Oh king, live forever!" (Dan. 6:21)—a very high blessing to seek on behalf of someone who gave him a death sentence less than twenty-four hours earlier. God is not dishonored, for if King Darius lives forever, it will be God who brings it to pass. God gets the credit for being the one able to do the work.

Gabriel is not stealing praise from God by singling out Mary for a commendation uttered to only one woman in all of human history, by saying, "Greetings, you who are highly favored! The Lord is with you" (Luke 1:28). He affirms her by (1) greeting her (a simple practice overlooked in many homes to the detriment of many relationships); (2) describing her as favored—she has earned nothing, can boast in nothing, and has passively received this bestowal, yet it is an honor to be savored, to be sure; and (3) declaring that the Lord is with her, for her, proactive on her behalf. Again, Mary is distinguished from all other women as being "favored," and yet ultimately God gets the honor, for he is the one doing the favoring, the gracing, the bestowing.

The writer of Hebrews 11 violates nothing of God's honor by commending the faith of Abel, Enoch, Noah, Abraham, Isaac, Jacob, Joseph, Moses' parents, Moses, Rahab, Gideon, Barak, Samson, Jephthah, David, Samuel, the prophets, and the martyrs. "For by it the people of old received their *commendation*" (Heb. 11:2). All of these were "commended through their faith . . ." (v. 39). They are commended, yet their commendation steals nothing from the glory of God, because they are commended for faith that is from him and in him.

In addition to the above, there are other instances of people being affirmed in the Bible:

- The Lord affirms Noah as righteous in his generation (Gen. 7:1).
- Pharaoh affirms Joseph as remarkably discerning and wise (Gen. 41:39).
- Boaz commends Ruth as a worthy (virtuous, strong, noble) woman (Ruth 3:11).
- Saul commends David for being more righteous than he (1 Sam. 24:17).
- Achish affirms David as blameless (1 Sam. 29:9).
- The woman recognizes that Elijah is godly and truthful (1 Kings 17:24).
- The centurion highly values his servant (Luke 7:2), and the elders affirm the centurion (Luke 7:4–5). Note that the centurion did not praise himself. Unsolicited praise from mouths other than the person's own is best, unless you are God, who may solicit all the praise he deserves.

- Paul commends Phoebe for her servant ways (Rom. 16:1–2).
- Paul commends the Corinthians for their faithful remembrance of traditions (1 Cor. 11:2).

Even to a bunch of scalawags, Paul affirms the work of God he sees in them:

> Paul, called by the will of God to be an apostle of Christ Jesus, and our brother Sosthenes,
>
> To the church of God that is in Corinth, to those *sanctified* in Christ Jesus, called to be saints together with all those who in every place call upon the name of our Lord Jesus Christ, both their Lord and ours:
>
> Grace to you and peace from God our Father and the Lord Jesus Christ.
>
> I give thanks to my God always for you because of the *grace of God that was given* you in Christ Jesus, that in every way you were *enriched in him in all speech and all knowledge*—even as *the testimony about Christ was confirmed among* you—so that you are *not lacking in any spiritual gift,* as you wait for the revealing of our Lord Jesus Christ, who will sustain you to the end, guiltless in the day of our Lord Jesus Christ. God is faithful, by whom you were called into the fellowship of his Son, Jesus Christ our Lord. (1 Cor. 1:1–9)

Paul had much to correct in the Corinthians. They had:

- serious doctrinal error
- divisions
- a form of immorality
- lawsuits among themselves
- problematic corporate gatherings
- misunderstandings and misuses of gifts
- broad opposition to Paul himself.

And yet, in his opening lines he tells them, "I give thanks to my God always for you." Why? "Because of the grace of God that was given you in Jesus Christ." Do you see the God-centered affirmation?

Jesus himself, the one to whom belongs all glory, affirms others:[2]

- He calls his disciples "salt" and "light" (Matt. 5:13–14).
- He says his listeners are more valuable than many sparrows (Matt. 10:31).
- He commends the woman of great faith (Matt. 15:28).
- He commends the woman of ill repute for doing a beautiful thing (Mark 14:6).
- He marvels at the faith of the centurion (Luke 7:9).
- He praises John with superlatives (Luke 7:28).
- He endorses the generosity of the widow (Luke 21:3–4).
- He commends Nathanael for not being a hypocrite (John 1:47).

Obedience as Praise

Obedience is a way of praising. Obedience honors the one being obeyed.

Obviously, when the Bible teaches us to obey God rather than man, it is not saying we should never obey man, children should never obey parents, students should never obey teachers, and drivers should never obey traffic officers. Generally, we are to obey those in authority. However, we are to disobey man when he is commanding us to do something that turns us away from God. Obedience to God supersedes obedience to man, but does not forbid all obedience to man.

17

In the same way, we ought to praise God rather than man, while acknowledging that the praise of God does not forbid all praise of others. It only prohibits the praise of others in ways that diminish God's glory, such as approving of their wicked practices, or making excuses for their sin, or attributing to them honor as though it is intrinsic to them and not derived from him.

What's the Point?

Good affirmations are God-centered, pointing to the image of God in a person. The only commendable attributes in people were given to them. Everything is from God, through God, and to God so that in all things—including the commendable qualities in people—he might get the glory: "'Who has given a gift to him that he might be repaid?' For from him and through him and to him are all things. To him be glory forever. Amen" (Rom. 11:35–36).

I remember being dismayed at the well-intended remarks of a seminary official at a large convocation who was about to thank a number of persons for their efforts. His intention and spirit were good. But he prefaced his thank-yous by saying, "The apostle Paul was always thanking people." Well, no, the apostle Paul wasn't. You will not find Paul doing such a thing in the Scriptures. He didn't thank people for things; he thanked *God* for people. Paul's practice is, "I thank *God* for you." Yes, the person is refreshed by the expression of gratitude, but God gets the glory. We are wise to give God-centered thank-yous and God-centered affirmations.

We've all heard of robbing Peter to pay Paul. We've also heard of robbing God by not paying tithes. I am suggesting that we rob God of praise by not pointing out his reflection in the people he has knit together in his image.

The best affirmation is rooted not only in the character of God, but in the gospel. The unspeakably good news of the gospel is that unworthy bankrupt sinners are invited to buy bread without money, to eat a banquet at no cost to them, purchased by Christ crucified who is himself their living bread. The good news is that cripples and invalids who cannot fight have a Champion who fights for them. The good news for law-breakers is that hearts of stone are replaced by hearts of flesh. The good news is that the sinner's justifying righteousness comes from outside him, from someone else. So does the source of his character. If a sinner develops good character, it comes from outside him. Common grace and saving grace abound. The goodness of gospel news is the magnificent beneficial overflow that comes from the God who is bountiful in mercy to sinners like me.

Salvation Is about the Person and Work of Christ— and So Is Character

Salvation is not in a code, but in a person. And so it is with character.

Just as salvation is not the keeping of an outward, superficial formula, or a recipe of good deeds, or a Religious Duty Check-list to be fulfilled by a person's exertion of will and effort, so character does not amount to an external set of guidelines to which one musters up conformity in his own strength and will-power. Rather, just as salvation is from Christ, through Christ, in Christ, and to Christ, so character is Christ's work emanating from within the believer and stemming from the vigorous life of the Spirit dwelling there. And in the case of the unbeliever, character is part of the common grace of God, as a gift to the individual.

Salvation is the work of Christ and character is the work of Christ. He does the work and he gets the glory.

God-centered affirmations point toward the echoes, shadows, and reality of a righteousness not intrinsic to the person being affirmed. These qualities are gifts, coming from outside people and being worked in them. Even without yet being fully complete, these qualities are nevertheless commendable, and are to be seen and highlighted. We can truthfully say to an unregenerate four-year-old, "God is helping you become more . . ." and fill in the blank with qualities such as: careful with your things (as a steward), cheerful around the house as a singer, cautious around dangerous things like hot stoves, and so on. While the child's growth in character is commended, God is identified as the source.

Before being able to affirm people well, we need to learn to affirm God, the source of everything to be affirmed in people. He is the source, the template, the standard. In order to be on the lookout for what is commendable in people, we should see the commendable in God. And for what should God be praised? "Praise him for his mighty deeds; praise him according to his excellent greatness!" (Ps. 150:2).

In simplified summary, we see here two things for which God is rightly to be commended: deeds that are mighty and greatness that is excellent.

First, while it would be idolatrous to erroneously praise people for being powerful if "powerful" is taken to mean an underived, self-generated potency, it is fitting to commend people for "mighty deeds," demonstrating God-given power to overcome things that should be overcome—things like bad habits, temptations, and falsehoods previously believed. It is a mighty deed to put to death sexual immorality, impurity, passion, evil desire, and covetousness, which is idolatry (Col. 3:5). Making progress in conquering such diabolical debilitations is commendable, a testimony to the grace and power of God in a person.

Second, praising people for excellent greatness is also fitting when we understand true greatness to be what Jesus explained it to be—serving in the strength God supplies and for which he gets the glory:

As each has received a gift, use it to serve one another, as good stewards of God's varied grace: whoever speaks, as one who speaks oracles of God; whoever serves, as one who serves by the strength that God supplies—in order that in everything God may be glorified through Jesus Christ. To him belong glory and dominion forever and ever. Amen. (1 Pet. 4:10–11)

We are stewards of grace. Those who steward well should be commended for it, and God should be praised for giving them the grace to steward the grace given. God is not given the praise he deserves when we ignore or deny the work he is doing in people.

Affirmation on the Way to Gospel Proclamation

Consider this: we risk damning others by not praising them. There are people around us in peril of hell unless we commend them. Isn't that kind of thinking idolatry? Is there anything to praise in the unregenerate person? Yes, the image of God. Our failure to praise them may unwittingly abandon them on their hell-bent path, even propel them on an accelerated descending trajectory, having alienated them from the very ones who possess the truth so crucial for them to hear.

Conversely, a great danger of relational evangelism is that Christians develop warm and open relationships with unbelievers, but fail to announce the claims and identity of Jesus.

Affirmation is a way to gain a hearing for the gospel.[3]

Affirming people gains a hearing so that we can tell them the most offensive news in the universe—God is angry at them (see Rom. 1:18). Our listeners will be more inclined to hear us if they believe *we're* not angry at them, but grateful for them. If *we're* not angry at them, they might be more inclined to listen to us when we tell them that God *is*.

One of the reasons we commend our little grandchildren when they do something commendable is so that we don't help harden them against the gospel, without which they will perish.

I found it helpful, for example, when interacting with a self-proclaimed atheist to take this approach: "I can see that you are an intelligent person. I'm inclined to think that you are interested in following the evidence wherever it goes, embracing reality, whatever it may be." Notice that I affirmed his ability to think, and gave him the benefit of the doubt that he has some measure of interest in the truth. "May I ask you to answer a question?"

Once granted permission to pose my question, I asked, "Would you be willing to describe the god you are pretty sure you don't believe in?" This question does several things. First, it affords me an opportunity to listen, which is both honoring to him and enlightening to me. Second, it elicits from him a clear articulation of just exactly what it is he denies, an exercise that helps me understand his mental obstacles and helps him rethink his own objections as he spells them out. After all, if we are going to have differences, it will be helpful to know exactly (and not merely imagine) where they lie. Third, it—surprisingly, to him—revealed common ground. You see the puzzled and startled look on their faces when I say to self-professed atheists who know I am a God-fearing Christian, "I don't believe in that god either." We still have a difference, and we both know it. But at this point, he knows I treat him with respect as a thinking human being and that we actually have some thinking in common. We have something in common to build on. I don't believe in *that* god either, but now he may want to know what kind of God I *do* believe in.

Heart Transformation

Notice the vital importance of God's transforming us so that we *become* the kind of person who affirms not as a chore, but as a delight. Heart transformation is God's work; the refreshment we desire to give others is also the work of God, as is our desire to give it. Just as love for a wife is not a chore but a joy in the transformed husband, affirming others is not a chore but a joy in the transformed affirmer. God is a desire-transformer. When he transforms our hearts, we don't affirm others out of sheer obligation, but rather because we want to. We want them to enjoy the refreshment from being affirmed that we enjoy when we are affirmed. God is the prime mover of all good affirming.

For example, before Saul underwent supernatural heart change, he wanted to murder Christians; but after, he rejoiced in the zeal of the believers (2 Cor. 7:7).

As a Way to Praise God, Praise Those Who Are Not God[4]

All commendation affirms something perceived as good by the one commending it. The person expressing jaw-popping awe at before-and-after pictures of the Mount Saint Helens volcano blast is praising not his own ability to gasp, but is pointing to the impressive powers unleashed, the massive volume of material heaved heavenward, the expansiveness of the space, the intricate convolution of resultant geologic formations, the rapid destruction and rapid regrowth of wildlife, and so on. Rightly understood, a person's commendations of power, scope, and material substance bend upward to the beauty and power of the source from which they come, the one who made them.

When the psalmist says, "The heavens declare the glory of God, and the sky above proclaims his handiwork" (Ps. 19:1), what are those heavens doing? They are declaring the glory of God. And what are those rock formations around Mount Saint Helens doing? They are declaring the glory of God. And what are those evidences of grace in your neighbor doing? They are declaring the glory of God.

Just as the heavens are declaring the glory of God, if only we have eyes to see it, when we commend the character of a person, we are also pointing to the glory of God from which that character is derived—if we have eyes to see it!

To fail to commend the character of Christ in people is to fall into the same lackluster indifference of a person who never exclaims what a beautiful morning it is, thereby robbing the Creator of glory he deserves for making that sky, that volcano, that character.

Accordingly—catch this—it is important when complimented to close the loop, to draw out the specific connection to God's work. Pass the compliment on to God. We honor God by responding to compliments by saying such things as, "God has been very gracious to me," or, "Any skill you see in me I received from God and through those he placed around me to train me," or, "You are very alert to notice what God is doing."

God gets glory by working in and through people: "All mine are yours, and yours are mine, and I am glorified *in them*" (John 17:10); "To this end we always pray for you, that our God may make you worthy of his calling and may fulfill every resolve for good and every work of faith by his power, so that the name of our Lord Jesus may be *glorified in you*, and you in him, according to the grace of our God and the Lord Jesus Christ" (2 Thess. 1:11–12). How is he glorified? By fulfilling every resolve for good and every work of faith. And how do we do it? By *his* power. Ultimately God gets glory through the goodness and faithfulness he grants his people. We should be noticing evidence of his grace and affirming it.

God-Pleasers or Man-Pleasers?

Children/spouses/workers should not become people-pleasers who crave approval in such a way that they will compromise on principle in order to get it. Rather, people *already do* seek approval (but often with defective motivations) and *should* seek approval (with God-honoring motivations), so give them approval for the

24

right things, for acting on godly principle and for not offending godly character. Encourage them as they seek to be workmen *approved* of God.

According to Matthew 25, we *should* desire to be commended (1) by God and (2) for doing good and being faithful. ("Well done, *good* and *faithful* servant." Goodness and faithfulness in Matthew 25:23 are the same two qualities affirmed in 2 Thess. 1:11–12.)

⤙ The elementary desire to be commended is not wrong. The desire to be commended becomes perverted when we desire to be praised for the wrong things, or when the desire to be praised is elevated above the glory of God in the good we do, or when we accept praise without the glad admission that the good we do is done in the strength that he supplies. (The One supplying the strength deserves the glory.) ⤙

Does everything I have stated so far seem like a damsel tied to the railroad tracks? Barreling down the tracks is a freight train of biblical observation from people like John Piper about to slam into affirmation:

> Our fatal error is believing that wanting to be happy means wanting to be made much of. It feels so good to be affirmed. But the good feeling is finally rooted in the worth of self, not the worth of God. This path to happiness is an illusion.[5]

So, is the refreshment of affirmation an illusion? How can I agree with Piper (and I do) when all along I've been saying that all of us want to be praised and we *should* want to be praised? The answer lies in whether we are praised

- for being like Christ,
- for doing good,
- for exemplifying a transformed life, and
- for making progress in holiness.

We should all want to be praised—by God himself!—*if* we are praised for the reasons mentioned above. God is committed to saying, "Well done!" He has promised to say it. He *desires* to say it. We should desire him to say it. To us!

Are you not eagerly longing to hear, "Well done, good and faithful servant!"? Something is seriously defective about the person who does not desire to be affirmed by God in this way: "Do your best to present yourself to God as one *approved*, a worker who has no need to be ashamed, rightly handling the word of truth" (2 Tim. 2:15).

The quest for such approval is no half-hearted affair. Do your best! Further, if we desire praise penultimately in order to bring glory to God ultimately, then we ought to fulfill the Golden Rule and award penultimate praise to others also for the glory of God. In the process, we give our loved ones a foretaste of glory divine. We fulfill the Golden Rule by saying "well done" to them, an imitation of the "well done" we want said to us when, in the strength God supplies, we do things worth approving.

Consider this text showing that when the Lord returns, he will come with commendation:

> Therefore do not pronounce judgment before the time, before the Lord comes, who will bring to light the things now hidden in darkness and will disclose the purposes of the heart. Then each one will receive his *commendation from God*. (1 Cor. 4:5)

Ultimately, all praise belongs to God. But penultimately, praise can and should go to people on the way to ultimately bringing glory to God, who gave those people the graces, gifts, and character they demonstrate.

And there's no question about the paradox here: pursue humility knowing that it leads to exaltation: "Humble yourselves before the Lord, and he will exalt you" (James 4:10).

Is It Wrong to Desire to Be Loved?

No. In fact, to *not* want to be loved by God is to be faithless, to expect God to act like something other than God. To be loved by God is good, and he gets the credit for being a glorious lover of the unlovely. In contrast, folly and sin conspire to make us desire to be made much of for our own sake only, thinking that we *deserve* to be loved. To make God a servile flatterer of our self-serving ego trip is idolatrous and deadly.

Similarly, it is not wrong to desire to be noticed, to be well thought of, to feel important, to be respected, to be recognized, to avoid conflict, to enjoy friendship, to have a good reputation, to be looked up to, to avoid the anger of someone, or to not suffer rejection—*if* our desire for such things is pure, meaning that God is seen as the Giver, the Root, the Fountain from which such things are flowing.

It's not wrong per se to desire:

- to be noticed, if we are letting our light so shine that when people see our good works they glorify our Father in heaven (Matt. 5:16).
- to avoid the anger of someone, if you are not cowardly but are courageously and faithfully leaving vengeance to the wrath of God (Rom. 12:18–19).
- to be well thought of, if we are approved of God (Rom. 14:18).
- to receive recognition, if we are recognized for having genuine faith (1 Cor. 11:19).
- to feel important, if we recognize we are making an important difference as instruments in the Redeemer's hands (1 Cor. 15:10).
- to be respected, if we are respected for fulfilling our God-given office in God-given strength (2 Cor. 8:16).
- to avoid conflict, if our peacemaking is not at the expense of principle (2 Cor. 13:10–11).

- to be looked up to, if we are esteemed highly because of our work in the Lord (1 Thess. 5:12–13).
- to have a good reputation, if our good name (which is better than great riches) reflects The Name (2 Thess. 1:11–12).
- to enjoy friendship, if friendship is first and foremost with God and all other friendships are for God (Heb. 6:10–12).

Therefore, I think Piper's statement remains true, with the insertion of one small word and a comma: "Our fatal error is believing that wanting to be happy means wanting to be made much of. It feels so good to be affirmed. But *when* the good feeling is finally rooted in the worth of self, not the worth of God, this path to happiness is an illusion." Do you see the insertion of the word *when*? Very often, the desire to be affirmed is rooted in the worth of self, and then it is diabolical and deadly. But the desire need not be rooted there. Sanctification supplies new roots. Transformed, we enjoy God's being made much of. It is not wrong to seek such happiness. In fact, it is crucial to seek such happiness.

Weeping and Hallelujah!
I pray desperately for wisdom and love, for they are far from my nature. I am a fool, and a selfish one. But I desire to grow in authentic Godlike wisdom and in genuine love. The desire itself is from God, or else I would not have it. And when on occasion I receive an unsolicited affirmation for having done something wise or having behaved as a loving man, my reaction is somewhere between joyful weeping and a speechless, *hallelujah!* Why weeping and why *hallelujah*? Weeping because I cannot boast. And *hallelujah* because I'm just so glad God is at work in me.

Do you see? He gets the glory for producing the quality being affirmed in me. I shouldn't stop desiring it.

Affirming Christlike transformation makes a distinction between praising a doer of good and praising a do-gooder. One commends the pursuit of that which is truly excellent; the other flatters the performer who longs to outdo others, seeking attention and man's applause.

Our problem then is not that we want to be made much of. Our problem is that we want to be made much of for the wrong reasons. Our problem is that we do not want strongly enough, desperately enough, to be made much of by God himself for reasons that he establishes and brings to completion in and through Christ and for his glory. We are nothing without him—but he has not abandoned us there.

Paul Boasts

There is *no* room for boasting in us. Yet:

> For our boast is this: the testimony of our conscience that we behaved in the world with simplicity and godly sincerity, not by earthly wisdom but by the grace of God, and supremely so toward you. (2 Cor. 1:12)

We should long to be affirmed as people who behave with simplicity and godly sincerity. Yes. Yes. A thousand times yes! Paul is boasting about his own behavior—but by the grace of God. The affirmation goes horizontally to people and vertically through them to God where it lands.

While a person values a paycheck, the true value is not in the check, but in an account held by one who guarantees it. Eventually the bearer must look beyond the check to where the real value lies. A negotiable check has momentary value, and once cashed, the canceled check serves as a testimony of a transaction made between one who is able to pay debts and one who held a debt that needed paying. Though a good check is honored, it's only honored momentarily, and then the real value is seen as being where it was all along: elsewhere. Affirmation of a recognized quality in a human hints at real quality in God who stands behind it.

Supremely Value the Supremely Valuable

Affirmation should not be a self-esteem free-for-all. Don't affirm any old thing. Don't affirm empty trendiness. Don't stroke the ego. Commend the commendable! Value the valuable! Supremely value the supremely valuable. Worship only Christ, and then commend his image in people.

If anything is to be commended in others, it is because in some measure they echo—even if faintly—the character of the One most worthy of praise, the One from whom all blessings and qualities flow. If anyone but Christ exemplifies any aspect of Christlikeness, it is because Christ enabled him to do it. Christ alone is sinless. Christ is Lord in an absolute way: no power exists except the power derived from Christ according to his own design. He made everything (Col. 1:16) and controls everything he made. He is transcendent and immanent, above and beyond everything he made and near to all he has made. Anyone but Christ who claims to be supreme is false, idolatrous, foolish, and damnable. There is salvation in none other. He wastes nothing he designs and he designs everything that is. That includes sinners who reflect him in greater and lesser degrees.

All the treasures of wisdom are in him (Col. 2:3). All authority in heaven and earth is his (Matt. 28:18). He is far above all other authority and power and dominion (Eph. 1:21). Therefore he is superior to angels (Heb. 1:4). He is greater than Moses (Heb. 3:3). Yet he looks upon the people with compassion (Matt. 9:36). Those who worship and love him, imitate him, reproducing his qualities, such as compassion (more about that in chap. 7). One reason worship of Christ is joyful is that he promises to use his unequaled attributes for the good of those who love and trust him. He is great *and* he is good.

Not only the power of affirmation, but *all* effective principles and dynamics are grounded in the God of the Bible. Emphasizing the power and importance of affirmation is not an effort to superimpose some kind of management practice or pop psychological technique over the Bible. The best management and relational practices have generally been borrowed from the Bible in the first place. If the world finds short-sighted, pragmatic benefits from affirming others, they are doing what worldly ideology has always done, co-opting biblical reality for twisted selfish aims. In spite of corruptions and perversions, the principles that order the world—including the worlds of management and psychology—are from God and reflect God.

Jesus is on a mission to receive praise (Matt. 19:28; Luke 4:15; John 8:54; 11:4; 12:23; 13:31–32; 17:1, 5; Acts 3:13), even if he has to get it from rocks (Luke 19:40). And the Father is passionate for his Son to receive praise—so passionate is the Father about such praise for his Son that his Son's praiseworthiness reverberates from those who resemble him in character. Paul translates that chain reaction into a command: "Be imitators of me, as I am of Christ" (1 Cor. 11:1). No glory is stolen from Christ when people imitate *Paul* this way. In fact, Christ's glory is magnified and multiplied.

Affirmation for Believers and Unbelievers

One way to state the purpose of life is this: Christlikeness (Rom. 8:28–29). We know that God works all things together for the good of those who love God, those he called and predestined to be conformed to the image of his Son. The best affirmations acknowledge and encourage progress in the direction that fulfills that very purpose for living on this earth: to glorify God by becoming Christlike. Admittedly, something may glorify God (like heavens and rocks) and not be Christlike in the way people can be. But if a person grows in Christlikeness, abiding in him by faith, that person *will* sooner or later glorify God—perhaps sooner *and* later.

To affirm Christlikeness in transformed believers is to affirm what Christ purchased with his own blood. He did not spill his blood for the church because she was worth it; his blood, spilled for her, *establishes* her worth.

To affirm Christlikeness in spiritually dead unbelievers is to recognize derived beauty. Yellowstone Park didn't make itself, yet we say, *Wow!* We say *wow*! in spite of the daily kill-or-be-killed rule of the jungle that is played out daily in the deep ravines and streams and forests of the park. In the same way that Yellowstone Park is a reflection of common grace, unregenerate persons reflect graces not intrinsic to themselves. To affirm the beauty of their character is to draw attention to the undeserved grace that God has bestowed upon them in the form of faint echoes of Jesus, even in the presence of as-of-yet unperfected flaws in those same individuals. In the providence of God, some unbelievers are actually better behaved than some believers. This behavior is God's gift to them, not their intrinsically meritorious character.

True, spiritually dead persons don't and can't practice obedience that comes from faith. But, when character is observed in a person—even in small baby steps—who's to say that faith has not already been given, and that we are seeing the early incremental evidences of sanctification underway? Certainly, we keep on looking for additional fruit, including a clear verbal testimony of confession, repentance, affirmations of truth, and denials of error. But it is a mistake to despise flickers of character as always bogus.

It is not our place to curse unbelievers. In warning us about cursing people, which is the opposite of affirming them, James wrote:

> For every kind of beast and bird, of reptile and sea creature, can be tamed and has been tamed by mankind, but no human being can tame the tongue. It is a restless evil, full of deadly poison. With it we bless our Lord and Father, and with it we curse people who are made *in the likeness of God.* (James 3:7–9)

The reason we ought not to curse people is that they are made in the image of God. In fact, we ought to affirm the likeness of God that we see in them (see chap. 7).

This might be the right moment to call the reader to join me in repentance:

> Lord, generally most of us do not imitate Christ as well as we should. While we rejoice that you are sanctifying us, having begun a good work in us, we nevertheless remain so far from Christlikeness in so many ways. We admit that there have even been times when we have behaved worse than our unbelieving neighbors. God, have mercy. Not only have we sinned in general, but specifically we have failed to commend the commendable. We receive from you the forgiveness that Jesus purchased for us on the cross, and we ask you now to accelerate our transformation into Christlikeness. Make us commendable and commenders of the commendable. For Christ's sake, so be it.

Key to Refreshing Relationships: The Simplicity

Oh, the power of affirmation!

Even though living at home, a fourteen-year-old young man had not spoken to his dad for two years—a painful estrangement for both of them. Under the same roof, they maneuvered around each other in anger, bewilderment, and deep disappointment, wondering, "Can't Christians do better than this?" I was teaching on the power and importance of affirmation to a group of Campus Crusade staff gathered from several states, and among the staff present was the lad's dad. After a break, the dad did not return.

Later that day, the man sought me out and explained why he missed the session. "I'm sorry I missed your next session. But after you talked about affirming, I went to the phone. I have a fourteen-year-old son who has not spoken to me for about two years. We used to fight about almost everything, and over time the fighting dissolved into a long, silent, uneasy truce. After being convicted by this teaching on affirmation, I called him, resolute that I was not going to criticize or correct him in any way, but praise him, because I do see things in him that are commendable. Well, this son who hasn't said boo to me in two years talked to me for forty-five minutes! I wasn't going to hang up. That's why I missed that session."

Just a few compliments unaccompanied by criticism opened up a relationship that had been closed for two years.

Oh, the avoidable pain I have witnessed (and caused) in relationships due to ignoring the one single practice this chapter will describe and prescribe. It's a universal principle of human relationships. It applies to everyone everywhere—adults, children, teens, males, females, easterners, westerners, Christians, non-Christians, in secular contexts, in churches, in classrooms, in offices. Not only does it apply, but we can't get away from it. We cannot escape its active force, any more than we can escape our skin.

This chapter recounts choices and changes real people have made in order to overcome heartbreak in tense, failing relationships—replacing God-belittling patterns with refreshing and God-honoring ones. I thank God that he has allowed me to join many others in rediscovering this door-opening key.

The Importance of a Key

We might not think a key is the main part of a building. The rooms, the roof, the walls, the doors, the windows, the square footage are more important than the key. But without the key, you can't have the rest. The key is crucial for gaining access. One night around midnight after the conclusion of an elder meeting, a fellow elder gave me a ride to my home where I discovered that I had no key, and my wife was away. There we were standing outside the house—I own it, I have "rights" to it, it's under my jurisdiction, it's fully assembled and ready to go, I'm longing for my bed in there, and I can't have any of it, because I don't have the key. So, my friend helped me break into my house by disassembling a window. Here's my point: if we forget this key to relationships, we not only may be closed out of those relationships, but it can feel to others like we are breaking in, like they are being violated, as in breaking and entering.

Similarly, the most important mechanical part of an automobile is not its key. Far more important are the power train, the wheels, the brakes, the steering mechanism. But without the key, the car is not available to the driver. It won't cooperate with his plans. Many people are puzzled as to why their relationships seem stuck and uncooperative, yet they are not putting the key in the ignition. Be encouraged that it's not too late to use the key.

One hundred percent of the soon-to-be-wed individuals I have surveyed do not expect to divorce the partner they are marrying. Further, they (and I) don't know of anyone who marries while thinking they will eventually be divorcing. Yet the statistics of lasting marriages fall far short of 100 percent. So what happens? Why do well-intentioned, optimistic, intelligent Christians with a can-do, hope-filled attitude fail? Millions go into marriages with good intentions, aspirations, hopes, and dreams, and then something happens; the closeness and cooperation evaporate. Invariably, such couples have misplaced this vital key.

When I speak of affirmation as the key, hear this: It is not the most important aspect of a relationship. For example, in a parenting relationship affirmation is not the most important thing parents will do for their children. There are things like feeding them, inoculating them, and teaching them the Bible. But without affirmation, well-fed, well-inoculated, well-instructed children may tune out their parents and their well-intended instruction—*especially* their instruction. Just as bedside manner is not the most important thing a doctor provides for his patients, without it patients may resist more important medicines and procedures.

Truth-telling is another parental provision more important than affirmation. But if we fail to affirm, our children may tune out the truth we are so interested in telling.

What Key?

Affirming others has clear biblical warrant.

> What then, brothers? When you come together, each one has a hymn, a lesson, a revelation, a tongue, or an interpretation. *Let all things be done for building up.* (1 Cor. 14:26)

> Let each of us please his neighbor for his good, *to build him up.* (Rom. 15:2)

While there can be multiple *im*plicit aims for pleasing a neighbor, the explicit aim in these texts is to build him up. Our marching orders are: "Build up your neighbor!" It's the Christian thing to do.

We have very good news: Our commission to build up our neighbor is not all duty and no delight. It is not all costs and no benefits. It is not all planting and no harvest, all preparation and no party.

On one occasion the apostle Paul reported the supernatural workings of refreshment and mercy this way:[1]

> May the Lord grant mercy to the household of Onesiphorus, for he often refreshed me and was not ashamed of my chains, but when he arrived in Rome he searched for me earnestly and found me—may the Lord grant him to find mercy from the Lord

on that Day!—and you well know all the service he rendered at Ephesus. (2 Tim. 1:16–18)

It is crucial to see that there are five parties in this text: (1) The Lord, (2) Onesiphorus, (3) Paul, (4) Onesiphorus's household, and (5) Timothy.

Try substituting the following parties:

1. In both the text and our substitution exercise, the Lord is the Lord.
2. Onesiphorus is you and me when we are refreshing others.
3. Paul is the others we are refreshing
4. Onesiphorus's household is the people who live with and around you and me.
5. Timothy is the onlookers who are observing you and me in our relationships.

Here, then, is a restatement of the text: God gives mercy to us and to those who live with us when we give refreshment to others, and in the process we are being observed by onlookers. Let's look a little closer at each of the parties.

First party: God is at work. Not once, but twice in the text God is explicitly named as a giver of mercy to the person who refreshes others. Don't miss this. While the fruit of *receiving* refreshment is of course refreshment to the one being refreshed, the fruit to the one *giving* the refreshment is mercy, and it comes from God. When we refresh others, God promises mercy to us!

Second party: Onesiphorus (you and me) is doing the work of refreshing someone else and in doing so will receive mercy from the Lord. Our work, our focus, our service is to refresh others. It's also our privilege. It is a service that gains a reward for the server.

Third party: Paul (the persons you and I refresh) receives refreshment. Refreshment is the commodity, and God has given us a supply to meet the demand. We should all desire to be people with a reputation for refreshing those around us.

Fourth party: Those who live with us are in a better (mercy-enriched) environment when we receive the mercy of God that comes from refreshing others.

Fifth party: As the recipient of Paul's letter, Timothy (onlookers) confirms the refreshment that is taking place. Onesiphorus is being watched, and so are we.[2]

Onesiphorus receives mercy as a consequence of refreshing Paul. You and I receive mercy as a consequence of refreshing others. Don't miss the connection between refreshing others and receiving mercy. God is proactive in a person's life when the person refreshes others. That factor alone should produce in us an eagerness to be a refresher, a cheerleader—a clear, strong, consistent, energy-giving affirmer of those around us! Do you want mercy from the Lord? Paul makes it clear that refreshing others and receiving mercy from God are linked.[3]

What is meant by "mercy"? What is the mercy that we receive when we refresh others? I will answer that generally and specifically. Generally, mercy is forbearing mitigation—release from a deserved punitive consequence, not getting what we deserve as a consequence of our sin and folly. Specifically, when God grants mercy to someone who refreshes others, the one doing the refreshing is released from the consequences he deserves for being a sinner in each and every relationship. For example, we don't deserve to have others forgive us, listen to us, or give us any second chances. Yet those things are mercy from God when we show our humble repentance by seeking to refresh, encourage, energize, and build up others, taking a genuinely loving interest in their welfare.

40

Our Calling: To Bless and Be Blessed

What does this refreshment look like and feel like? Imagine: You're stacking hay bales on a scorching summer day in Uncle Guy's barn loft where it's very hot indeed and dusty and itchy and stifling with the smell of pigeon poop and twine and sweat dripping everywhere, and there's not a dustless breath of air to breathe. At last the final bale comes up the conveyor from the hay wagon and the tractor shuts off and the machinery clamor grows quiet; climbing out the second story hay door and feeling the fresh, dustless, relatively cool air, you go to the shade tree on the lawn where Aunt Florence is serving lemonade on ice. Ahh. Affirmation is like an invigorating sudsy shower after a long day of manual labor. It's like a cool rain after a long, hot dry spell. It delivers a combination of relief, respite, hope, optimism, satisfaction, and energy. It's life-giving. It blesses.

Blessing others is the very calling of the Christian: "Do not repay evil for evil or reviling for reviling, but on the contrary, bless, for to this you were called, that you may obtain a blessing" (1 Pet. 3:9). Again notice the multiple parties involved: (1) You, blessing somebody else, (2) somebody else, receiving your blessing, and (3) God, blessing you for blessing somebody else. To this you were *called*. I am using the terms "blessing" and "affirmation" synonymously here. Later we will see a distinction: while not all blessings come in the form of affirmations, all God-centered affirmations are blessings.

How does Jesus handle the woman caught in adultery in John 8? She is apprehended in the act of adultery, and her prosecutors, ready to stone her, bring her to Jesus for his verdict. Jesus stoops to write on the floor of the temple, briefly addresses the scribes and Pharisees, and stoops to write again as one by one they leave, starting with the eldest. Jesus is left with the woman. Remember, she is guilty of a capital offense. She is caught. What does Jesus say? While he does not sweep her sin under the rug, *first* he rescues her, makes the environment safe for her (v. 7). He will get around to saying, "Sin no more," but *first* he makes clear that condemnation is not the agenda. He doesn't begin with correction.

Part of God's mercy to us when we refresh others is the boomerang effect he has designed into the universe: "He who refreshes others will himself be refreshed" (Prov. 11:25 NIV).

It is the law of the harvest: we reap what we sow. Do you want your relationships to be more refreshing to *you?* Then serve up banquets of refreshment for *others*. Note: God (not others) is the ultimate source of our refreshment. When we refresh others, the refreshment that we receive, ultimately coming from God, may not come from them, but from somewhere else that God has appointed: "And whoever in the name of a disciple gives to one of these little ones even a cup of cold water to drink, truly I say to you, he shall not lose his reward" (Matt. 10:42 NASB). Where does the reward come from? Not from the little ones, but from God. God is the rewarder of those who refresh others.

And now let us go a little deeper.

The Affirmation Ratio
On the face of it, nothing could be of less use to a person than to take up a book about something he already knows how to do. But alas, we often turn away from doing what we know.

I assume that people know how to affirm in a thousand ways, often without giving it a thought. For example, all of the couples in my premarriage classes through the years have become couples as a direct result of practicing affirmation, wittingly or unwittingly—though probably wittingly. We all know how to do it. We know how to show another person we notice them. We make eye contact. We speak to them in uplifting ways. We touch them in welcoming, affirming, safe ways. We share stories, laughing even at *attempts* to be lighthearted or funny. We bring them gifts. We draw them into a smaller and smaller circle from which others are excluded, in the process giving them our house keys, our car keys, our computer password, our school locker combination—things that say, "I've welcomed you into an inner circle with exclusive membership." Such privileges can be very affirming. We share secrets, which affirms in the same way. And here's a big one: we know how to interrupt what we are doing when the other person shows up. We just drop what we're doing. This says, "You're more important to me than these other things." We know the verbals and nonverbals that say, "Yes! I approve!"

I have asked premarriage classes, "When one of you discovered what your partner's favorite color is, did you do anything with that?" One guy told me what happened after he mentioned to his fiancé that he liked orange shirts: "I have lots of orange shirts." His fiancé didn't own stock in an orange dye company or anything. She bought the shirts simply because and *only* because she discovered that he preferred them. His wish became her happy command.

I've asked those classes, "When you discovered that your fiancé had a favorite restaurant or favorite food, did you do anything with that information?" Of course! They carried out plans to go there or to prepare that dish. Such gestures say, "I'm alert to you and to what refreshes you, and it gives me pleasure to refresh you in the ways you like to be refreshed." We affirm and refresh others by paying attention to them. There are infinitely more important things than orange shirts and favorite foods, things like the character qualities we find in Jesus Christ. My point is simply to show that we already know how to affirm; the challenge is to practice the process consistently and in God-centered ways.

Salesmen are typically good at affirming people early in a relationship. "It's so nice to meet you! I can tell you are a person with distinguishing taste. You'll appreciate this model! Oh, you don't like this particular model? I can tell you are a person with distinguishing taste." The risk for us is that a salesman has a built-in incentive to extract something from us, and may therefore compromise our welfare to make a sale. The importance of the salesman's reward may outweigh our refreshment. This is self-centered manipulation, and Paul is not talking about that to Timothy. Onesiphorus is not selling Paul anything.

It seems easier to practice affirmation early in relationships, and it can get harder later. Have you ever noticed in a restaurant that some couples are talkative and some are not? What happened? Generally, new relationships are still predominately affirming, but as relationships endure the years, they also endure a lot of correction. More specifically, affirmation didn't keep up. Not enough affirmation was dished out compared with all the other messages in the relationship. A fire not stoked goes out. A refrigerator unplugged rots the eggs, which were perfectly good not too long ago. A garden not tended erupts with weeds, not vegetables. Affirmation is the fire-stoking, refrigerator-electrifying, garden-tending side of relationships.

The Importance of Proportionality

Generally, it is easy to affirm early in a relationship, because no offenses have been committed yet. But over the course of time, we can experience a growing desire to bring certain corrections to the table. Which will dominate? Affirmation or correction?

Proportionality matters when it comes to affirmation, for affirmation can be choked out by criticism, correction, or mere indifference and neglect. How much affirmation is enough? There's no magic number. Picture a horizontal line representing a continuum from a healthy diet of affirmation on one end to an insufficient quantity on the other. The affirmation in any given relationship can be plotted along the line.

←————————————————————————→

Insufficient Affirmation   Plenty of Healthy Affirmation

The same relationship can be plotted along a line with the same meaning, but with different labels.

←————————————————————————→

Correction Dominates   Correction Is Counterbalanced
                                          with Affirmation

Picture human relationships as ships on water. The natural winds blow them toward the left of the continuum. Wise people give intentional proactive energy to pulling relationships toward the right.

The aim is not to find the precise point on the line that is justifiable, but to unmistakably (in the eyes of the people around us) move toward the right. Robust proportionality between affirmation and correction may vary from relationship to relationship, and may even vary from season to season within the same relationship. Sometimes women send signals that they desire a little more refreshment during seasons such as pregnancy or mothering young children. Sometimes men take criticism more severely when they are running late or feel they are being made to run late by someone else. The point is not to calculate some once-and-for-all ratio, but to be actively refreshing.

This is where we get in trouble: affirmations tend to evaporate over time. Meanwhile, corrections keep piling up. Corrections tend to out-number affirmations, and by doing so, corrections sabotage or undercut the value of affirmations. Occasions to correct keep arriving like a Mobius treadmill in perpetual motion. "You left the lights on in the car, dear." "Finish your homework, son." "Late again?" "Not that way; this way." Individually, these are innocuous, and one might argue, necessary. But they pile up, and if not counterbalanced by an overwhelming gang of affirmations, they take over the flavor of the relationship. One hair in a casserole may not even be noticed, yet enough hair will result in choking. Some will choke even at the *thought* of hair in their food; similarly, people may emotionally choke at the thought of any more correction coming from us.

The importance of affirmation does not entirely remove the place of correction. We're going to live with sinners. We're going to marry a sinner. Our children will be sinners. Our parents are sinners. The people around us are going to pull boneheaded moves, and in love it will sometimes be our place to point them out. They are going to smell bad, and it's our job to inform them before they go out in public. They will burn the burgers. They will do something that is mediocre, that will hurt the team or waste household finances, or something else regrettable. But love does not look first for ways to correct.

Think this way: give so many affirmations as a pattern, a way of life, that you gain a reputation for it. You are known for your affirmations, not your criticisms, your corrections. In Acts 4:36 Barnabas is called the "son of encouragement." What's *my* reputation? Mr. Crabby Pants? Old Lady Battle-Axe? Miss Nit-Pick? We should unleash so many affirmations that those around us lose track. So, it's not a matter of mathematical precision. It's not a strict algebraic formula but a spiritually organic way of living, more like romance than rocket science, less like knitting (with its relentless counting: knit one, purl two), more like the weather—how much rain is enough? Well, that depends on how dry it's been. And what are you trying to grow—a watermelon or a cactus?

According to one perspective, "It takes more than one positive to overcome a negative. You hurt my feelings, so do something nice for me. Are we okay? Not usually yet. The bean counters are telling us that a healthy state in a system actually requires 3–5 positive events to overcome one negative event."[4]

In his devotional at one of our pastors and wives retreats, John Piper told us that C. J. Mahaney tells his staff "three for every one," meaning three affirmations for every criticism. When I asked C. J. about that, he said, "Yep, three identifications of evidences of grace for every corrective observation or expression of humor where someone is the object of that humor. And that is just for the Pastors College students who are together each day. For the spouse, parent, pastor, church member I would want the ratio to be more like five to one or ten to one."[5]

As Alex Chediak writes, "Not only would [a robust affirmation ratio] tend towards softening the tone of the rare critique, but it ensures that the critical remark is heard in a larger context of love and delight."[6]

A guy might be thinking, "This doesn't come easy for me. I'm not good at it. It's not natural for me." But men who desire mercy from God get busy refreshing their wives. You can decide to affirm. God will help you. You can dedicate yourself to it: "With God as my help, I *am* going to do this. I'm going to make a joyful project out of it." You can tackle the mountain (the whole marriage relationship) and break it down into a bunch of easy-to-climb molehills of affirmation.

But we must not be surprised in this fallen world if we encounter obstacles.

Corrections Weigh More Than Affirmations

The drag that corrections have on a relationship is compounded by the fact that they already outweigh affirmations—they have greater impact individually. The sting of a rebuke outweighs the fresh whiff of a bouquet. A person sniffing the flowers when a bee stings quickly forgets the flowers even if the bouquet is very large. If a pattern of corrections is outweighing the affirmations, the sting stays with us, and the corrections keep picking the scab.

It takes many affirmations to overcome the impact of a criticism, because criticisms are heavier and sting more. Worse than a bee sting, criticism can be like a sword thrust: "There is one whose rash words are like sword thrusts, but the tongue of the wise brings healing" (Prov. 12:18).

When the Bible describes some words as sword thrusts, we are helped to understand how painful words outweigh healing words. It simply won't do, when a sword wound has been inflicted, to put salve and a bandage on the wound for one minute, or one hour, or one day. It takes more time to heal than to wound. So it is with affirmations and corrections. It can take a lot of affirmations to heal a particularly painful correction, even if the correction was as necessary as the wound from an emergency appendectomy.

It's easier for a person to endure physical sickness than the crushing blows of words that impact the soul: "A man's spirit will endure sickness, but a crushed spirit who can bear?" (Prov. 18:14).

Two Clarifications

First, self-interest is not selfishness. Everyone knows that to seek gain by means of someone else's loss is wrong-headed. But if you seek to be rewarded by enriching someone, that is not selfish. Your reward for their enrichment is not selfish on your part, even though your reward for doing it is in your *self-interest*. Rewards are a big deal in God's economy. You can't even come to God unless you believe that he rewards: "And without faith it is impossible to please him, for whoever would draw near to God must believe that he exists and that he rewards those who seek him" (Heb. 11:6).

If you invest in your marriage by refreshing your wife and in God's mercy he makes your marriage a sweet and fulfilling one, it is not selfish of you to have refreshed your wife. She still

48

gets the refreshment, even if you get to join her in enjoying a good marriage. If you refresh your teens and in God's mercy he makes your kinship solid and genial, it is not selfish for you to have refreshed your offspring. They still get the refreshment while you both enjoy a happier home life.

Second, though we benefit from refreshing others, the refreshment is theirs and is to be real refreshment: "Each of us is to please his neighbor for *his* good, to his edification" (Rom. 15:2 NASB).

It won't do to offer what we assume is refreshment, if it doesn't really refresh. The man who buys his wife a power saw for Christmas may not be refreshing her, having failed to look at the gesture through her lenses. You may think it refreshing, but if the recipient of your gesture doesn't find it refreshing, it isn't refreshment. Home-baked bread may seem like a nice gift, but if your friend is gluten intolerant, the bread doesn't refresh, even though the gesture is well-intended. Some men take their wives to sporting events thinking that the wife will enjoy the sport as much as they. The Greek philosopher Bion put the problem this way, "Though boys throw stones at frogs in sport, the frogs do not die in sport but in earnest." The Lord can give us transformed loving hearts enabling us to get behind the eyes of our children, our spouse, our employees, and so on.

Apply this second caution to behaviors such as sarcasm. "I was just funnin'." Well, if it isn't fun for them, it isn't fun. It isn't refreshing, it's depleting. When I was a boy, a man in our church would catch me and tickle me. Even though it would start with me laughing and giggling, I was desperate to catch my breath, to escape—and at least once I cried. Because of the early laughter, he mistook the exercise as a game. It was no game to me. I was not refreshed. I started to avoid him. Though he thought the tickling was playful fun, the frog was dying.

Why Mess with This Affirmation/Correction Business?

Answer: because it's already messing with us. If an overly corrective under-affirming pattern continues, three things can happen:
First, *others stop hearing our corrections*. After all, nothing they
do gets rid of the static, so they turn down the inner volume
control. Our latest correction just blends in with the pile built
up by the conveyor belt of corrections coming their way from
us. Our best advice given with the best of intentions simply
goes in one hardened ear and out the other.

Second, *they stop hearing us altogether, not just our corrections,
but us as persons*. They wouldn't ask us the time of day. If they
were to ask us the time of day, they fear they may hear, "Did
you misplace your watch again? The clock is right there on the
wall." They aren't interested in another sword thrust from us.
Having turned down their radio to avoid the static, they hear
none of our messages at all.

An overabundance of correction will result not only in a
person's tuning out your legitimate corrections, but tuning you
out almost altogether. Proportionality skewed toward correction
that leads to this second outcome—namely, that your counterpart stops listening to you—is pictured in Jesus' teaching
about the speck and the log. First get the *huge* log out, and
then you will see better to be able to help your brother with
his *tiny* speck, and your brother won't have your hypocrisy to
deal with. Similarly, first get your affirmations up, and then you
might win your brother's ear for your corrections, your efforts
to work on his speck.

One signal that a person has tuned you out is when lightheart-
edness has gone out of the relationship. One Sunday morning
after speaking to a class of parents and teens who had invited
me to teach on this subject, one of the moms approached me. As
we talked about our experiences, we observed that in a relationship where there is not enough affirmation, there is no humor.

The light-heartedness drains out. While loving relationships are not all about tomfoolery, people who can't laugh together are probably very thirsty for more affirmation in the warp and woof of life together. Take laughlessness as a clue, as a cue to ratchet up the affirmation.[7]

Synonymous with tuning out is withdrawal. For example, a lot of husbands simply withdraw as a result of the drip, drip, drip from the leaky faucet of correction from their wives. I'm not excusing withdrawal, just observing it. Men ought not to withdraw. But they don't want to fight with their wives, and they may not know what to say to them, or know what the rules are for fair fighting, or know where the boundaries are, so instead of verbal jousting they go out and mow the lawn or sweep the garage or walk the dog. Don't do it, men. And women, you can help draw them out by keeping an eye on your pattern of affirmations and criticisms. And your tone of voice.[8]

When the magnitude of bulldozing correction continues to bury affirmation, then a third effect results: *the relationship itself becomes oppositional*, like a bad echo that repeats what you say, but with disagreement. For example, imagine in the evening you say something like, "It's getting late; perhaps we should fix some supper."

But your counterpart replies, "I'm tired. I don't know if I have the energy to fix anything."

"Well then, how about we go out to grab something? Or order out?"

"That's expensive, and you know it's getting late in the month, and we're trying to get ahead on our bills."

Do you see how everything being suggested is countered? A relationship severely damaged by neglect of the affirmation ratio can get to the point where our counterparts are against our suggestions simply because they come from us.

Affirmation and Correction Are Like a Bank Account

There's an economy to affirmation, a ratio. Just as there is an affirmation ratio in the political science of elections (differentiating between an election outcome that's a mandate and one that's a squeaker) there are ratios in the affairs of the heart. Proportionality matters.

The ratio is like a checking account. Affirmations are deposits. Corrections are checks you write against the balance in the account. If you write too many checks in relation to the deposits, your checks bounce—they're no good. It will take additional deposits to restore your credit. And if the pattern of writing bad checks continues, you'll not only face overdrafts and fees and penalties and bounced checks that don't buy anything, but your account may be frozen until you get serious about putting things in the black. Your checks may be refused at certain businesses, regardless of your restored balance with the bank. These establishments may no longer wish to do business with you; your record with them is too problematic. And if your pattern of writing bad checks continues, you may be arrested and removed from circulation altogether.

What I have just described coincides with the three outcomes of too much correction compared with affirmation. First, not accepting specific input; then, not accepting your input at all; and third, opposition to any position you take on nearly any subject.

Withdrawals from the checking account include legitimate corrections and all criticism, including name-calling, sarcasm, and blaming. Even more inert and benign things like silence and withdrawal can deplete the checking account, like service fees that fail to get entered in the check register.

The good news is that even if your relationship has reached the third stage (oppositional), you can dig out of the hole you are in and reach a place where the other party will actually invite your opinion. Instead of frozen out, you're invited in! You become "safe" as a sounding board when people know the first thing out of your mouth will not be criticism when you hear their ideas. Legitimate criticism is important, even crucial, but your counterparts eventually won't be interested in your wisdom if they have tuned you out from the diet of criticism you serve up.

When you first begin to restore a pattern of affirmation to a relationship, the other person may not believe you, or receive affirmation well from you. That's because of the deficit. Your checking account is in the hole. But steady affirmation can unlock the gridlock in the long run. How long? It depends in part on how big the deficit is.

Practical Suggestions
To reverse the trend of an overly corrective relationship, try the following:

1. If she has stopped listening to you, quit preaching.
2. Stop moralizing about listening: "You should be listening to me!" Instead, ask the Holy Spirit to do *his* job.
3. Affirm. Stay up nights if you have to, thinking of ways to say what is so commendable in him.
4. Keep up a steady, tender flow of words and gestures that confirm and commend them.
5. Model. We don't affirm any particular quality we don't personally embrace and exemplify in some appreciable measure. If we try to commend punctuality while always running late ourselves, our hypocritical compliments become off-putting.
6. Love the unchanged person as is. Be a blessing to that person *before* he listens to you.

I repeat: things are moving in the right direction when affirmation, not correction, is the *pattern*. Relationships are healthy when so much affirmation is being spread around that no one is keeping track of either affirmation or correction, because the relationship doesn't feel predominately demanding, but refreshing. This is not a matter of a raw mathematical ratio, but a perception from the other person's point of view. This requires us to see things through others' eyes. Do *they* see us as affirming?

A shortage of affirmation explains many things, from teenage rebellion to failed marriages. Affirmation withers up, and with it, the relationship. Meanwhile, ongoing corrections make the relationship more and more painful. Consider gang behavior. The young person may find he gets no commendation from the adults in his life, but when he spray paints the bridge, the gang howls with delight. Guess who has influence on him? Or the wife generally seems critical, but that secretary at work is understanding and affirming. Who is gaining influence with the husband?

Persons who are drained by depression may find a key here. One of the things a depressed person needs is mercy, and when the depressed person by faith opens his mouth and affirms *others*, mercy from the Lord is on the way.

The Principle Is Simple

The affirmation ratio is about earning a hearing. There are going to be times when, in love, you are going to want people to hear you, to understand, to listen, to get it. Here then is the simple principle: people are influenced by those who praise them. Giving praise does wonders for the other person's sense of hearing.

Some readers' antennae are perking up, and they are thinking, "Wait a minute. This is sounding a lot like humanistic, man-centered, self-esteem psycho-idolatry." Don't misunderstand me. Persons more holy and wise than I have talked about the importance of praising people. Puritan writer Richard Baxter said, "They love those who best esteem them highest. The faults of these admirers can be extenuated and easily forgiven. [my insertion: Isn't that what you want? To be easily forgiven?] . . . If you would have his favor, let him hear that you have magnified him behind his back and that you honor him. . . ."[9]

When John Calvin says, "We readily believe those whom we know to be desirous of our welfare," he connects hearing with manifest goodwill.[10]

Informal idioms speak of the affirmation ratio this way: "You catch more flies with honey than with vinegar." Or: "A spoonful of sugar helps the medicine go down."

Let me tell you how my failure to affirm took my fathering relationship to the brink.

Affirmation Is Pivotal at Home

I thank God for the way in which my relationship with one of my daughters was rescued and strengthened. When she turned eleven, she was suddenly aloof and unapproachable. Up until then she had been very pleasant, but overnight she became disinterested in relating to me while remaining interested in relating to others.

My daughter no longer listened to me. She didn't seem upset or angry, just detached and uninterested, as though her relational radio no longer picked up my frequency. Or maybe she was *intentionally* not tuning in. Or both. I wasn't the first person to agonize in a painful state of affairs with someone—a spouse, a loved one, a coworker, somebody at church. The lines were dead. You keep dialing the number, but nobody picks up. I felt I was losing her.

All of a sudden, seemingly overnight, it was as though all the knowledge of the universe had instantaneously been transferred to her brain and she no longer needed to listen to anyone. In that same instant, all of her parents' knowledge had been sucked out of their brains leaving them with nothing of value to say to her. Of course, it isn't really true that she knew everything, and her parents knew nothing. But that seemed to be her perception, and it put her in a dangerous place. It was obvious to me that if nothing were to change, the relational drain that had gained a foothold would accelerate into the deadening and deafening silence of alienation.

How could we help her, this child of our love? We couldn't get to her heart. She was taking her cues elsewhere and we were locked out. Meanwhile, we looked around and saw other young teens also cutting off their parents. I recall that near the end of his five-year *Why Wait?* campaign for sexual purity, Josh McDowell was asked by an interviewer if he could sum up five years of programing aimed at equipping youngsters around the country to avoid huge and regrettable mistakes. In one sentence, what was the point? McDowell replied, "It comes down to a quest for daddy's arms." He meant that young girls who do not receive genuine love from their dads will settle for cheap imitations in the arms of those who are all too willing to exchange flattery for favors, feigned affection for physical privileges. An eleven-year-old who tunes out her dad is in a very vulnerable place. My love for my daughter couldn't resign and just leave her there.

Daughters who are eleven are going to need some input, even corrective input, from their dads, input without which they will be at a severe disadvantage. Love obligates a dad to not give up when a child tunes him out. I soberly thought that I must regain a hearing.

I determined that this eleven-year-old daughter whom I loved would receive more praise from me than from anyone else on the face of the globe. I became a student of her. I thought, if I have to stay up nights thinking of ways to commend her, then I will, because she's going to need to hear her father (who happens to be me).

So I began following her around. I don't mean two steps behind her, but I was always on the lookout for things to commend. Alert affirmation requires vigilance.

One day, she was in her room with her door open, so I knocked and entered. It would be helpful at this point to contrast her with her sister at that time. Her sister was very orderly: her shoes were all in pairs on racks, her clothes were all hung up, a place for everything and everything in its place. But the daughter that I'm talking about used an MBO method (Management by Observation): leave things out where you can see them.

As I entered her room that day, I noticed that she had arranged the items on the top of her dresser in such a way that the taller things were in the back row, and shorter things were stair-stepped toward the front, so that you could see everything. If you place shorter items in the back, you can't see them, and you have to reach over the taller things in front to get to them, risking knocking over taller items in front when reaching past them.

I exclaimed, "I *like* what you've done here! You're methodical. This makes complete sense. Very orderly. Very systematized. I see the character of God in this. Jesus does *everything* decently and in order, and your orderliness reflects the way he is." And with that, I walked out, ignoring the rest of the tsunami in her room.

Only a few minutes later, I happened to walk past the kitchen when she was hugging her mom. I immediately stopped, shook a pair of touchdown celebration fists in the air, and declared, "I *love* what you're doing! It is so *good* for an eleven-year-old to be hugging her mom! It's good for the young woman. It's good for the mom. It's good for the dad who happens to walk past. And I think it pleases God himself!" Is it okay to bring God into our compliments? If you don't think so, then you're going to have a hard time with this book. Bringing God into compliments is the *best* way to give them. I do not mean bringing him in as an afterthought, but *basing* your compliments and affirmations on his character.

I made affirming her my responsibility (which it is). I kept up the barrage of affirmations, and in a matter of days we had our daughter back. To this very day she asks our opinion about lots of things, things she would certainly be at liberty to do without checking with us. The channels of communication are open and sweet.

Do we think she's perfect? No. For one thing, she is cut from the same fabric as her dad, so she's a sinner, like her parents. But we find pleasure in affirming positive behaviors, which then become positive patterns, because behaviors that are consistently rewarded tend to be repeated. This daughter is now married with children, and she is a *very* orderly homemaker and affirmer of her own children and husband.

Affirmation Clicks in the Classroom

I saw the rebellion-breaking power of affirmation as a public school teacher. I had a verbal agreement with the administration of the public school where I taught sixth grade for seven years: I wanted all the fatherless sixth-grade boys to be assigned to my classroom. I may not be the perfect male role model, but all the other teachers were female, and I hope it's true that I'm a better *male* role model than any of the female teachers on staff.

One of those students, Wayne (not his real name), was particularly problematic. He would damage the school property, carving up the furniture. If you sat ahead of him he might write on you or on your clothes; he might cut your hair or your clothing. He once took a cube-shaped eraser and drove stick pins through it in every direction so that the sharp ends protruded like a Sputnik satellite, and then he would toss it at someone and say, "Catch!" If you caught it, you'd bleed. Even if you *didn't* catch it, you might bleed.

Wayne was in affirmation deprivation, for understandable reasons. He was a poor student, so he didn't receive any academic accolades. He wasn't athletic or musical. He came from a broken home and was socially not easy for his peers to be around. He wasn't receiving praise anywhere for anything. In my classroom, I positioned his desk closest to my own, so I could more readily keep an eye on him.

Wayne was in my class, and I was his teacher. I wanted him to listen to me, to hear me, so I prayed, *Lord, what can I affirm in order to gain a hearing? Is there some small approximation of a God-honoring trait upon which I can capitalize for Wayne's refreshment and for the good of the class?*

One day, I had assigned some work to the students, and I was circulating through the classroom helping those who requested assistance. Out of the corner of my eye, which was almost always on Wayne, I noticed that he wasn't doing his work, but he wasn't killing anybody, either. He was daydreaming, gazing out the window with his chin in his hand. "I'll take it!" I thought.

So I maneuvered behind Wayne and laid my hand on his shoulder. His head immediately jerked around, and he leaned slightly away as if to say, "What did I do *now?*"

I said, "Wayne, I can tell you're deep in thought. I like that about a guy. I like a man who's a thinker!" I can still see the look on his face, at once bewildered and yet savoring it like no pleasure he could remember experiencing. His face said, "So *that's* what a compliment feels like." And with that, I patted him on the back, and resumed my rounds, still keeping an eye on him.

He had been affirmed for doing something God does—think. God himself invites us to reason together.

Wayne still wasn't doing his assigned work, but at least he was moving in my direction. His eyes were following me around the room, and whenever he saw that I was about to turn in his direction, he would quickly snap into the chin-in-hand posture of *The Thinker*. Affirmation tasted so good that he was lining up for seconds. What was happening? His hatred for teachers was being undercut, because he was affirmed by one.

Affirmation has power to gain a hearing for the affirmer even in the ears of the outright rebellious. Perhaps that hearing is one form of the mercy that comes from God toward the one doing the refreshing.

Following our breakthrough, did Wayne immediately take off in his academics and become valedictorian? No, and that wasn't my immediate aim. On the way to getting him to cooperate in doing his studies, I aimed at getting him to cooperate at all, to just listen to me. We can affirm progress, even when it still falls short of mastery. Sometimes we thank God for increments. I had Wayne as a student for only one year, and affirmation helped us move our relationship in the right direction.

Affirmation for a More Merry Marriage

I received a long-distance phone call from a wife who underscored the savory atmosphere in her home because of her husband's simple and straightforward application of the affirmation principle. I had explained the power and importance of affirmation at a men's retreat on a Saturday, and on Monday this wife of a hog farmer who had attended called me.

"Keep on teaching men what you taught at the men's retreat," she cheerily pled.

"What do you mean?"

"That stuff about affirming."

"Why? Is something good happening?"

She replied with an overflowing enthusiasm, "It's wonderful!" She explained how her husband was out doing chores and suddenly thought of the breakfast she had served him. He reached into his overall pocket, made a note, and went about his business. Later he was thinking about the cute pigtail holders in the hair of his three young daughters, made a note, and returned to his work. When he came in for lunch he placed his note scrap next to the sink where he could read it while washing up, and started in: "You know, I don't think I thanked you for that breakfast; I was still thinking about it in the middle of the morning. And those cute little hair thingies you put in the girls' hair? I don't know what they're called, I wouldn't know where to buy 'em, or how to put 'em in, but I sure think they're cute. What's for lunch?" as he continued washing and drying his hands. Nothing especially suave, romantic, or clever. Just noticing. Just alert and faithful to follow through. And it meant so much to the wife that she made a long-distance phone call to affirm it.

Don't you like to be appreciated for what *you* do? Then practice the Golden Rule, and appreciate others for what *they* do. Affirmation is what love does, doing unto others as would be desired if the shoe were on the other foot. Even God seeks affirmation, and gives it. His commending of others is in accord with the fact that God keeps his own rules, including the Golden Rule.[11]

Many couples wonder why the shine has gone off their diamond, when in fact refreshment has gone off the menu. Refreshing your spouse will also help affair-proof your marriage. Without the refreshment that comes through affirmation, affections shift subtly. Affairs start with a polite listening ear, somebody sensitive, and soon the affirmed dish has run away with the spoon.

These concepts are a reminder, and given their simplicity we are easily tempted to think we already *do* remember them. But do we?

Lord, help us act on what we know. Refresh others through our affirmations. Mobilize us to bless that we may obtain a blessing.

Affirmation is rewarding. The next chapter offers four ways to make affirmations more powerful and nine rewards for doing it.

Toward Greater Refreshment: The Complexity

"And let us consider how to stir up one another to love and good works." (Heb. 10:24)

By focusing on affirmation this book is focusing on just one key to refresh relationships, and focusing on only one key is simple. But the key itself, the thing receiving our focused attention, is not simple. The key is complicated.

For example, there is one key to my car. It opens the doors, opens the trunk, opens the glove box, turns on the accessories, and fires up the ignition. One key—that's not complicated. It's small, lightweight, and fits in my pocket. But the key itself is a marvel of engineering. Not only does it possess an array of cuts, grooves, and protrusions along its shank, an easily gripped handle for turning, and a well-designed hole for the key ring, but it also contains electronic wizardry—a chip—that works with the car's computer system to synchronize with the designer's security measures. It's a complicated key. When our house was broken into and our car keys were stolen, it took several days' pay to replace the keys. The complications make the keys expensive, so don't lose them. Similarly, don't lose track of affirmation; it, too, is a costly key to replace, once lost.

Four Characteristics of Good Affirmations
Detached from Correction

A person reading to this point might falsely conclude, "I have a loving correction that would be wise to make, and I understand the power and importance of affirmation, so I'll stir in a few affirmations with my correction." Correction packaged with the affirmation will contaminate and weaken the affirmation, perhaps making it altogether fruitless.

Accordingly, it doesn't work well to save up future affirmations, thinking, for example, that you want to speak with your husband about throwing his dirty socks on the floor, so you quickly rattle off a series of compliments like, "Thanks for paying the bills, shoveling snow off the walks, and I see you shaved today. Now, about your socks . . ." Corrections tend to cancel affirmations, and the closer the proximity to correction, the more crippled the affirmation.

I once heard about a manager who unfortunately used something he called the "sandwich method" on his employees. He used affirmations as bookends around his criticisms. When he desired to correct one of his employees about something, he would first start with a proverbial slice of sandwich bread, affirming something in that employee such as, "I'm glad that a diligent worker like you is on our team." Then he would insert the sandwich filling: his correction, something such as, "But the quality of your production isn't up to our standards." And then he would finish up with the other slice of sandwich bread, another affirmation such as, "So keep up the good hustle while we improve the quality." Well, his clever, observant employees began to see the pattern: the only time he affirmed was when he was also going to correct. And so when he began complimenting one of them, what do you think they were doing in their minds? You're right if you think they were battening down the hatches, making sure the forward shields were locked on, diving into emotional foxholes and taking cover. Then, when he delivered the correction, they would absorb the sting, the sword thrust. And finally, during the follow-up affirmation, the second slice of bread, the employee's silent self-talk had already run toward self-justifications, like, "Well, the quality would improve if management provided better materials," or, "You have us on such a tight timeline, we can't keep up the pace," or, "I just haven't been myself since the dog died, since my quadruple amputation, and since my teenage son bought a bazooka," so that the employee doesn't even hear the follow-up affirmation. The workers tuned out the manager. It is not difficult to see one of the reasons why his affirmations seemed not very affirming to them.

It was a sandwich all right, and he boasted about his method, but his employees began to call it the baloney sandwich.[1] Let affirmations stand alone, separated from correction.

Steady

Related to the first observation (affirmation is better if unattached to correction), this observation goes farther. Even if there is no correction at all, there must be a steady stream of affirmations. Indifference and passive silence do not honor. A vacuum of approval is not likely to refresh the person or to glorify God who has graced the person. Just because we don't drink poison doesn't mean the body will be healthy; it must also receive nutrients. Just because we aren't drilling any holes in the bottom of our canoe doesn't mean that the waves and storms of life won't require us to actively do some bailing from time to time. A steady diet of affirmations in a relationship is like watering and hoeing in a garden—it's refreshing and keeps the weeds down. Just doing nothing won't keep the weeds down. Weeds have a way. It's part of this fallen, cursed world.

It is a foolish error to assume that because I don't beat my wife, don't swear at my kids, and don't shoplift from area merchants that I'm neighborly. Affirmation goes beyond passive acceptance to a steady diet of active approval, not aiming only for minimal correction, but earnest commendation.

Giving affirmation requires time, so make time for it. Make time for it serendipitously on the spur of the moment by interrupting what you are doing in order draw attention to some commendable action, and make time for it by planning it into your schedule. Do things like setting aside some time this coming Sunday afternoon (make an appointment with yourself) to jot an affirming note to your pastor. Put affirmation on your calendar—for example, at 10:00 tomorrow morning, I'm calling my wife from work just to say that I thank God for her faithfulness to me. Regarding that friend's upcoming birthday (birthdays are not serendipitous, but are like clockwork, allowing us to plan ahead), decide ahead of time to block out enough time to write the qualities you appreciate in your friend.

For over twenty-five years I have daily written my wife a note (two sides of a three-by-five card). Though it would be foolish of me to assume that a single regular practice like that will suffice as the sum total of a healthy rhythm of affirmations flowing toward Vicki from her husband; nevertheless it is one way to keep a stream of "I love yous" and other positive messages coming her direction. She has collected shoe boxes full of them. Though we've lost count of the number of notes, one could do the math. Unfortunately, this deeply flawed husband still fails at adequately affirming Vicki from time to time, by fixing my attention on some aspect or other of her behavior that I would like to see changed. But when the focus goes there, on changing her, it's not long before I'm no longer a bringer of refreshment to her, and I can tell it. Regret soon follows. God, who is faithful even when we are not, awakens me, and I strive to re-establish a joyful drumbeat of genuine affirmations toward the long-suffering and forgiving wife he has given me. The three-by-five cards are simply one way of trying to keep the diet of affirmation steady.

There's probably not a person reading this book who is thinking, "Affirmation is stupid. I'm not going to do this." However, if we think we should be doing it, then why aren't we? The absence or sparseness of our commendations is generally not because we jump out of our chair one sunny afternoon and announce, "No more affirmations from me! No sirree." Instead, we become preoccupied, distracted. Life happens—the baby needs changing, the phone is ringing, and we told the neighbors we'd help them put together the thingamajig. And before we know it, a lot of drifting water has passed under the bridge, the weeds of indifference have grown, and we can't remember when we last passed out the blessings. The slowdown in affirmation is exacerbated if there's been a tiff or two mixed in, further chilling the air. Let a book like this serve as a wake-up, a reminder, a goad.

Yesterday's refreshment doesn't refresh permanently. You can't stockpile freshness.

And those who wish to establish healthy patterns of affirmation don't wait for an invitation.

Creative readers will no doubt develop their own ways of keeping up a healthy pace and volume of God-glorifying affir-

don't wait for Kyle & Kari to call

mations that refresh those around them, and I would be grateful
to hear about them.

Honest

Commend only the commendable. It simply won't do to make
up phony commendations. Not all the children in Lake Wobe-
gon are above average, and it's laughable to think they are. So
don't call your husband the wisest man in the world, unless you
really think he is. (If you think he is, then you should tell him
so, thanking God along the way.)

If affirmations are not true, they will not truly refresh, and
they won't last for long. They won't really build up, because
they are lies. They deceive. They will be found out, and a sense
of refreshment will be replaced with a sense of betrayal and
distrust: "Truthful lips endure forever, but a lying tongue is but
for a moment" (Prov. 12:19); "The getting of treasures by a lying
tongue is *a fleeting vapor* and a snare of death" (Prov. 21:6).

Such deception is not what this book is advocating. When
affirmations are disingenuous, the affirmed will come to not
trust the affirmer and will begin to wonder what's really going
on. Phony affirmations backfire sooner or later. A manipulative
agenda can't hide behind false affirmations any more than you
can play hide-and-seek in a glass house. Phony affirmation is not
only deceitful, but hateful: "Whoever hates *disguises himself with
his lips* and harbors deceit in his heart" (Prov. 26:24). Did you
see it? Whoever *hates*!

True affirmations are more likely to come out of a truly
affirming heart, which is another reason why it's so important
to be going hard after God, working out our salvation with fear
and trembling, pursuing holiness, and asking God to transform
us from the inside out. Gordon Cheng put it well: "People who
genuinely encourage other people are not putting it on. It comes
out of who they are—or better, who God has made them."[2]

this is my goal, it is genuine

God-Centered

The aim is to glorify God by refreshing people as we help them see God at work in their lives, moving them toward Christlikeness.

We help people be shallow when we focus our compliments on their braiding of hair, wearing of gold, putting on of clothing, sequins, piercings, and tattoos (see 1 Pet. 3:3–4). Such things are external. Rather, let us pay attention to patterns of character that emerge from the work of God going on inside a person. We'll give more attention to character in chapter 7.

God-centeredness is why I commended my eleven-year-old daughter for things like being orderly (orderliness reflects the most orderly being in existence: God) and not for having a dresser top that looked "nice" or some other vague compliment. There are dozens of ways you can spot the image of God, even in unbelievers. When I commended my student Wayne for being a thinker, I recognize that God is the greatest thinker in existence. "Come, let us reason together," God says.

So, look for Godly things to commend, without flattery or manipulation (subjects we explore in chap. 5). In doing so, we're pointing to something very valuable, and we're saying, "I see it in you! I value *it* and the God who is the source of it." Pointing to Christlike character qualities in a person is a way of praising God, by commending his attributes reproduced in others by his grace. By valuing a character quality, we attribute honor to its source. And we can be explicit by stating it plainly.

I enjoy commending young people and children by pointing to some aspect of Christlikeness and saying, "You are Christlike [in some specific way], and I want to be like you in the way you are like Jesus." For one thing, it seems to have significant positive influence in a youngster's thinking to receive earnest praise from an adult. For another, they have nothing to boast about, for it is Christ I am commending in them ultimately, for no one possesses any measure of Christlikeness unless they received it as a gift. "For who sees anything different in you? What do you have that you did not receive? If then you received it, why do you boast as if you did not receive it?" (1 Cor. 4:7). For a third thing, it is biblical for Christians to imitate Christlike people as they imitate Christ. "Be imitators of me, as I am of Christ" (1 Cor. 11:1).

So make your commendations more about character than things like "you're so cute." Cute is a weak compliment. Cute comes and cute goes, and for most of us it's well on its way out. Physical beauty is fleeting. By the time we're old, we're going to sag and bag and our teeth are going to yellow and we'll be gray and walk with a limp, and we'll probably have some measure of many features that are not attractive. But a compliment such as, "You sure take good care of your health," highlights responsible stewardship, which is a character issue. While there is nothing wrong per se in complimenting a smile, it is better to commend cheerfulness.

Even when someone fails in his performance, there are ways to commend good character. Again, these have to be honest affirmations, commending only what is commendable. But when the casserole is burnt, we can commend the creativity and courage it took to experiment with that new recipe. When the child breaks the window, we can commend him for the honesty to tell us about it. When somebody owns up to an error or a mistake or an accident, we can commend her humility in confessing it or her sense of responsibility in owning up to her actions. Even though depravity reaches every aspect of our humanity, we still are not as thoroughly bad as we could be. The image of God is not totally eradicated from us. Even Hitler did not kill his mother, and he came up with a number of inventions useful to this day. The foremost sinner (Saul; 1 Tim. 1:15) could be commended for his (misplaced) zeal (which God would eventually harness and channel in a fruitful direction) in the same way that he later commended the unbelieving Romans for their zeal: "I bear them witness that they have a zeal for God, but not according to knowledge" (Rom. 10:2). Paul says the Romans' zeal for God is not according to knowledge; so he goes to work on the defective knowledge (by writing the letter to the Romans, for one thing), but not without affirming their zeal. They were defective, yet commended nonetheless.

Is There a Place for Upholding Standards?

Rarely, but sometimes—when there is a deep, deep deficit—it might be wise to consider a temporary moratorium on correction altogether for a season. I say rarely, because in a fallen world love must exhort and rebuke when doing so is best. Love does not permanently suspend all correction. Correction is one of the things that love does. A friend will wound a friend: "Faithful are the wounds of a friend; profuse are the kisses of an enemy" (Prov. 27:6).

There are times when love simply must protest. How long should a moratorium on correction last? Until the relationship shows improvement, moving away from being oppositional and moving toward tuning back in, or until there is an absolutely life-threatening emergency—"Get out! The house is on fire!"—or until the moratorium critically compromises the fulfillment of the responsibilities that come with one's jurisdiction. A great warden might commend model prisoners while not handing over the keys to the prison.

Even though many relationships fall into conflict or deadness over lack of agreement on standards, affirmation is not about lowering standards. It is about commending incremental progress toward those standards as those standards reflect the character of Christ. In commending my recalcitrant student Wayne for thinking, I was not abandoning his responsibility

71

to do his studies. I was helping him take incremental steps toward them.

If keeping up a steady diet of honest, God-centered affirmations that are detached from correction is starting to seem complicated and difficult, why bother? Consider the following nine benefits.

Why Affirm Others?

1. Affirming others earns us the right standing from which to make suggestions. It gains us a hearing. This benefit is so rich and life-giving. I earnestly desire for people to get this, and practice it. How sad and desperate are the relationships that have needlessly deteriorated for lack of affirmation. The needless anguish I have observed (and experienced) in relationships is among my main motivations for writing a book like this. The general rule: people are more willing to listen to us when they have experienced the refreshment of affirmation from us. Oh, the needless pain we experience and cause when we dismiss this too quickly.

2. Affirmation lifts morale. It's good for the home, the office, the church, the locker room. As I was at work on this book, a staff member who knew what I was writing e-mailed me, telling of how one simple affirmation from a coworker had made her day. Why wouldn't we want to make a person's day? Especially if a few words will do it!

We are energized by appreciation, even if it's only for making the attempt, even if the project itself failed. Don't you like to be appreciated for your effort, even if the project wasn't a complete triumph? People around us like to be appreciated that way, too.

3. Affirmation energizes people. It not only lifts their spirits but motivates them to action. Affirmation not only points toward character already being demonstrated, but it fosters more of the

same. Persons who may have given up, thinking, *what's the use?* are refreshed to take another run at it.

Chuck Swindoll is right: "No question about it, affirmation spurs us on. It fuels our inner fire. It deepens our determination."[3]

4. Affirmation of others makes us easier to live with. Solomonic wisdom warns us that "it is better to live in a corner of the housetop than in a house shared with a quarrelsome wife" (Prov. 21:9). It's not that quarrels will never happen, but Solomon is speaking about a kind of wife for whom quarrelsomeness, not affirmation, is a pattern, a way of life. Solomon describes such a wife as dripping.

How does a faucet acquire a reputation for being a dripping one? Answer: the pattern. A faucet that drips, but rarely, gets no reputation as a dripping faucet; a rarely dripping faucet gains a reputation as a source of refreshment. It's the pattern, the predominance, the proportionality that feeds the reputation. And understand that our dripping corrections, complaints, criticisms, and suggestions for improvement can feel as torturous to others as "Chinese water torture" feels to its victims. Neither water torture nor criticism leaves a physical mark, but both can drive a person bonkers, making him desperate to escape the one who assaults with dripping. Consistently commending the commendable helps us be refreshing fountains and not dripping faucets.

The dripping faucet could attempt to make the self-justifying argument that each drip is meant as refreshment and, in fact, actually does contain refreshment. But if the water doesn't get inside, it only assaults, becoming a torment.

5. Striving to affirm others puts us in the practice of looking at them positively—that is, looking for evidence of God's work in them. Affirmation changes us before it changes them. It is one of the more beautiful features that God has designed into this

fallen world, namely, that no one can sincerely benefit another without benefiting himself.

I can be so quick to point out the negative while taking the positive for granted, assuming people around me will behave the way I think they should and forgetting that I might have a role to play in *encouraging* them to behave in certain ways. We become preoccupied by the chores of marriage, children, jobs, church, and pets, and we lose sight of God's purpose for *everything* in this life—to conform us to the image of Jesus (Rom. 8:28–29). We so easily move away from being on the lookout for the life of Christ in our counterparts.

Look out the window: what are those heavens out there doing? They're declaring the glory of God. But worship is aroused only in those who have eyes to see it! And now look at your neighbor, your spouse, your child, your parent, your coworker, your pastor. Do you see God's glory there? The image of God is present in all humans, but is often missed by those not looking for it.

Affirmation doesn't require deep insight, just simple sight. And action. See good things and point them out with appreciation.

6. Affirmation constructively uses time that could have been wasted complaining. Many of the corrections from our mouths are not constructive and up-building, but are simply complaints, raw grumbling. Whether we grumble or we speak affirmation, the heavenly cameras are rolling: "Do not grumble against one another, brothers, so that you may not be judged; behold, the Judge is standing at the door" (James 5:9).

Furthermore, many of the complaints we make aren't worth the effort. Let it go. Let it be. Let it die: "The beginning of strife is like letting out water, so quit before the quarrel breaks out" (Prov. 17:14).

To nitpick is to chip away at a dam. The wise quit chipping before the dam breaks. There are times in certain disputes when

I know that I know I am right, with God and his host of angels as my witnesses. But the issue simply isn't worth the energy it will take to correct it and the draining impact it will have on the relationship. When is an issue important enough to correct? See appendix 1 on the decision grid.

7. By commending Christlike qualities, and celebrating them when we spot them, affirmation showcases the character of God, giving him honor for being the kind of God he is. Andy Stanley adds, "Celebration reinforces a value. . . ."[4] By affirming, we teach. We make explicit what is important. To paraphrase James, show me your values without affirming, and I will show you my values by affirming (see James 2:18). Do we value the image and character of God in people? Then let's affirm those things in them.

8. Behaviors that are rewarded and celebrated are more likely to be repeated. So reward what you'd like to see more of. It's basic Psychology 101. It's even basic dog training. You say "Sit," the dog sits, and you give the dog a treat as reinforcement. You're going to get more obedient sitting. If every time you reach out to hug me, I poke you in the eye with a sharp stick, pretty soon you stop trying to hug me. If every time the teenager walks in the door, he hears things like, "You're late again. Wipe your shoes. Don't just toss your jacket on the chair; hang it up," he starts to associate coming home with conflict, criticism, and pain—and he loses an appetite for coming home. Years ago when I was a college student, back in the day when a coin could actually buy something, some of my friends and I were at a restaurant and decided to place a coin on the table as an added gratuity every time our server came to our table. After just a few trips, she caught on. By the end of our meal we had forty or fifty coins stacked up—yes, she made that many trips. Rewards matter. They incentivize. The word *incentive* comes from a Latin word

that means "set the tune." Wouldn't you like to set the tune in your relationships? Use affirmation.

9. When we commend God's image in people, God is glorified, and that's why we were made—to glorify God. Isn't it unspeakably good that we get the pleasure of fulfillment simply by doing what we were created to do? God gets the honor when we affirm his qualities we esteem, and we get the satisfaction of esteeming and enjoying those qualities, and pointing them out.

When we affirm God's character in people around us, not only are we *talking* about character, we are actually *exemplifying* one aspect of God's character. Blessing others reflects the image of the Christian's Father. It's what Christians do, because it's what the Father does. He even makes the sun rise on the good *and* on the evil, and sends the rain on the just *and* on the unjust: "But I say to you, Love your enemies and pray for those who persecute you, *so that* you may be the sons of your Father who is in heaven. For he makes his sun rise on the evil and on the good, and sends rain on the just and on the unjust" (Matt. 5:44–45).

Power of Affirmation in Navigating Controversy

On a very cold Minnesota winter morning I was bundled thick against the icy Canadian wind as I marched with several thousand others to mark the anniversary of *Roe v. Wade*. The march route was adorned by occasional pro-choice protesters with large placards chiding our pro-life efforts as being antiwoman. The setting was cold not only meteorologically speaking, but the air was chilled with icy looks and cold shoulders. In one part of the march a shouting match had erupted and it was ugly. It seemed to me that the pro-life marcher did a particularly poor job of winning friends and influencing people, and a pretty good job of making all of us marching with him appear to be angry, rude ruffians.

Continuing the march and seeing one particularly large and provocative placard, I felt the impulse to ask its guardians about it, but thought it would only erupt into a charged argument, and so I walked on by. Ten minutes or so later, I thought, "No. I'm going to speak with them," and so I returned to the placard's double guards, one of whom would not look at me or acknowledge my presence in any way. He looked off in the distance, literally stiff-necked. It had to be pretty hard work for him to ignore me and avoid me. And hard work it is when affirmation runs thin in relationships.

"May I ask about your placard?" I queried with a genuinely respectful tone, for these were human beings made in the image of God. There is more than one good way to jump-start an awkward relationship, and "May I ask you a question?" is one good way. Like a British Royal Guard, the one continued not to make eye contact with me and didn't even twitch; to him I did not exist except as a threat to his placard and mission. But the second fella said, "Well, what?" (meaning, what's your question?).

I took it as an invitation to continue. In strained relationships it can be very important to not proceed without an invitation, like playing "Captain, May I?" or "Simon Says." Show deference to the captain and heedful respect to Simon. "I'm noticing your placard, here. I don't know who designed it, but its graphics are strikingly attractive and its message is powerful." There were no words on it, just a huge rendering of a coat hanger encircled with a slash through it. It was a graphic not hastily thrown together by some amateur, but was colorful and simple, and though we were on opposite sides of a controversial issue, I could affirm the graphic skill. So I did. And then I took another figurative step forward, "I take your poster to mean that you oppose self-inflicted coat hanger abortions, am I right?" In tense situations, it can be good to not jump to conclusions, even when you're pretty sure you already understand what the other side means. Slowing down to confirm the other party's meaning is another way of affirming them as human beings who might like the opportunity to correct *me* if I have misunderstood. I am not beyond the possibility of misunderstanding, a healthy and humble admission to make. "Right," he replied, meaning that his poster was explicitly against coat hanger abortions.

Proceeding, I said, "Well, I think we have something that you and I can enthusiastically agree on." He looked at me as though I had forgotten which side of the issue I was marching on. "We both are in favor of the safety of women. We are men, and the safety of women is important to us, even though we aren't women ourselves. I appreciate your willingness to come out here on a very cold day, seeking to protect women from a procedure that will never threaten you personally. That seems altruistic to me." I'm not sure that he understood the word "altruistic," but I *am* sure he took it as a compliment, which it was.

"May I ask another question?" While his sidekick still stood stiff as a poker, this man was opening up to me. By asking permission to pose another question instead of just charging forward, the conversation was kept from shutting down, like the shouting match that had erupted elsewhere on the march route. "Sure," he replied. The first time I asked permission to ask a question, he gave me a tentative "Well, what?" because he was uncertain about what I might do. In response to my second request to interview him further, he replied casually with a "Sure." The cold was thawing. The door was opening.

So I asked my next question: "Could you tell me how many women have been injured by coat hanger abortions? Do you have that information, or could you point me to somebody who does?" His stammering response was something like, "Hmm . . . nooo . . . no, I don't." His pokerfaced partner offered nothing, not even a flinch. "I suppose you could check at the library or somewhere," was the best he could do. He wanted to help me do my research and get the facts. He was warming up.

On to my next question, "Well, can you tell me how many women have been injured by *legal* abortions in medical facilities?" Same answer: "Hmm . . . nooo . . . no, I don't, uh, have that information. I would think you might be able to get it at a library, or you could try to go online."

He's conversant now, and I moved on to my last question: "What do you say to the person who *does* have that information—the person who knows approximately how many women have been injured by coat hanger abortions in the United States and how many young women have been injured by legal abortions—what do you say to the person who has that information and knows that the number of woman injured by coat hanger abortions is less than one percent of the women who have been injured by legal abortions?" Checkmate. He looked embarrassed, which is appropriate. He hung his head and looked at the ground. But he wasn't angry, not with *me*. That is, he didn't see me as his opponent; he saw the data as his opponent. He was awakening. Do you see how affirmation—looking for something to commend—opened the door to talk about the issue that divided us? And he was backing away from his hard stance. His partner walked off, having never said a word; we won't win them all, and the practice of affirmation is no ironclad guarantee. Our conversation ended when the public address system fired up and the rally program began.

I hasten here to say that beautiful graphics should not be used in the service of killing defenseless children. But if I had started my conversation there, I suspect our discussion would have quickly gone in the direction of the shouting match. My goal isn't just to protest, but to persuade.

Real Life Written into Totally Fictitious Cinema

I debated with myself whether this book should make reference to fiction, especially such spiritually fallacious fiction as Star Wars, in order to illustrate the point of this book. I am not mainly concerned here with fictional characters like the emperor and Darth Vader, even though they have become iconic in the world of cinema. My point is that the writer, George Lucas (who is not a fictional character), in order to make his outrageously fictitious characters seem realistic, employs the power of affirmation.

Lucas seemed to understand the powerful influence of praise when he wrote the third Star Wars episode, *Revenge of the Sith*, in which the evil emperor, Senator Palpatine, seduces Anakin Skywalker to the dark side of the force by praising him with a string of affirmations, which steadily influence Anakin. How does Anakin get sucked into the evil emperor's dark scheme? Notice these affirmations which I've collected (omitting other portions of the conversation), simple comments of praise that keep drawing young Anakin, winning him.

PALPATINE: The council doesn't seem to fully appreciate your talents.

PALPATINE: They know your power will be too strong to control.

PALPATINE: You've been searching for a life greater than that of an ordinary Jedi . . . a life of significance, of conscience.

PALPATINE: I can feel your anger. It gives you focus, makes you stronger. [Even though the evil emperor commends evil, the commendation has its influential effect.]

PALPATINE: You have great wisdom, Anakin.

ANAKIN: I will do whatever you ask.

PALPATINE: Good.

ANAKIN: I pledge myself to your teachings. To the ways of the Sith.

DARTH SIDIOUS: Good. Good. The Force is strong with you. A powerful Sith you will become.

ANAKIN: The traitors have been taken care of, Lord Sidious.

DARTH SIDIOUS: Good . . . good . . . You have done well, my new apprentice. Do you feel your power growing?

ANAKIN: Yes, my Master.

<u>Praise has tremendous potential as an ally to persuasion</u>, and we should not forget it. Just as the Jedi council forfeits influence in Anakin's life by criticizing him without affirmation, while the sinister Palpatine gains influence through praise, divided families lose track of the tremendous power and importance of simply affirming.

As long as I have digressed into the world of cinema, let me quote Samuel Goldwyn, the filmmaker, who is widely known to have advocated, "When someone does something good, applaud! You will make two people happy!"

If it helps you, think of it this way: geese honk encouragement and fly in formation. Skunks travel alone.

By now, alert readers discern that my arguments about the power and importance of affirmation rely on several assumptions. In the next brief chapter, I will make some of the crucial ones explicit.

4

Important Assumptions

Several important assumptions underly the assertions I make about the power and importance of affirmation. Some readers don't need this chapter, and they are welcome to skip it. Others have begun to wonder if I have taken into consideration several important matters I have not yet mentioned. This chapter is for such readers.

Here then are five crucial assumptions.

God Sovereignly Brings about Ends through Means

If God wants you to understand the content of this book, he can simply zap your brain, and voila! you get it. But he is more likely to deliver understanding of this book by means of having your eyes pass back and forth over the page, after first having spent time learning to read, and before that learning to sit up, use your thumbs, etc. In addition to ordaining the end (understanding and practicing the content of this book), God ordains the *means to* the end (reading it). God appoints effects, and he also appoints the causes that bring about those effects. Prior to delicious raisins, he ordains roots and rain and sunshine and grapes. He ordains that certain behaviors will bring predictable consequences (ask the man whose thumb has met his hammer).

God could achieve refreshment in the lives of people around you without your participation, but that's not *how* he has planned such refreshment should come to pass in the lives of those who know you. He could wave his hand and get instantaneous results, but he often seems to glory in working through complex processes: Joseph is a slave and prisoner for thirteen years; the children of Israel wander in the wilderness for forty years; the prophets foretell of the Messiah for hundreds of years, and at long last the long-awaited Deliverer arrives. God is bringing about ends through means. The God of the miracle is also the same God who works through natural processes. He could just snap his fingers, and refreshment would happen. But he ordains that refreshment be achieved through means. The means I am talking about is your affirmation of others, affirming them, blessing them, commending and congratulating them, and thanking them. Those actions on your part are the means, and if you subtract the means, you won't get the end: relationships in which the people who know you are refreshed. This book will focus on means, while granting that God brings about both the ends and the means.

Could we just pray, asking God to refresh people directly? Sure. And he might do it. He certainly can. Meanwhile, I'm assuming that the cause-and-effect relationship between affirmation and refreshment is still in force.

We Are Dependent upon the Spirit
How can we affirm people who often do things we vehemently disapprove of? People we loved and enjoyed when the relation-

ship started can eventually become a pain in the neck. The pain of relationships impedes and destroys even the *desire* to affirm, much less the active practice of affirming. A day sometimes comes when the other party is frankly unbearable, and we don't want to put up with them any longer, much less affirm them. At that point, the weary natural self won't do; the self needs help, divine help. Utter dependence upon the Holy Spirit is assumed in this book, though I won't give much attention to it in these pages.

If all a person possesses are concepts and information, but not life, then he will fail to love, fail to affirm well, and only confirm his own guilt, failing to do what he knows he ought to do—namely, affirm in love.

Though the preponderance of this book is not about spiritual dynamics related to being filled with the Holy Spirit, I'm assuming it. Spirit-filled Christians will be *able* to do, and will *want* to do, the things we will talk about in this book. Non-Christians may or may not. People who are not Christians might be attracted to the power of affirming of others initially, but affirmation takes grace and eventually the temptation to snipe will rise. Faithful, steady affirming of others requires taking up a cross, and taking up a cross goes against human nature. So we must rely on the Holy Spirit, abiding in Christ. Abiding in Christ is the lifeline to steadfast love. How precarious it is to turn away from the Holy Spirit, thinking that consistent affirmation can be done in the flesh, especially when what we are talking about in this book is God-centered affirmation.

Furthermore, the very character of Christ that I am emphasizing cannot be produced by the flesh or some kind of behavioral reward system, and it cannot be manipulated or engineered by following a cookbook. It is the result of supernatural transformation. Having said as much, as dependent as Christlikeness is upon the life of Christ being within a person, the process of sanctification can be nurtured and refreshed by God-ordained affirmation he calls us to deliver in the strength he supplies.

Love Affirms; It Also Corrects

This book emphasizes the part of love that affirms, but does not deny the part of love that corrects. In love, we owe correction to one another: "But exhort one another every day, as long as it is called 'today,' that none of you may be hardened by the deceitfulness of sin" (Heb. 3:13).

There's a time when love gets in the loved one's face with correction. While such correction can be done gently and tactfully, it must be done and not abandoned altogether as though love never confronts. Love offers correction, but that's a topic for a different book.

Everything Can't Be Said in One Book

This small volume won't exhaust everything relevant to the subject at hand. In fact, other writers will be able to say it better, more completely, and more compellingly, and I would be happy if they would do so. Relationships would be better off for it.

In chapter 6 I will try to address some of the more prevalent questions elicited by the five earlier chapters. Meanwhile, I admit that not every conceivable question will be addressed.

Even in this very chapter about assumptions, not every relevant assumption is discussed. So if you think something important has been omitted in this book, you're probably right.

Context Matters

"A word fitly spoken is like apples of gold in a setting of silver" (Prov. 25:11).

What makes a word "fitly" spoken? Truthfulness is not the only aspect of fitness. Fitness hinges upon many things such as tone, facial expression, body language, timing, motive, and more—including the context of what you are saying. Someone who enters a conversation already begun is wise to wonder, what else has been said already? Context matters.

Take, for example, the simple sentence, "Hail, King of the Jews!" Whether it is "fitly" spoken hinges upon whether it comes out of the mouths of children lining a path with palm branches or from soldiers who have just flogged an innocent man, mounted a twisted crown of thorns on his head, and mocked him. Same words, different (opposite) meaning, based upon context.

I argue in this book that some of your most reasonable and truthful and important statements will be rendered fruitless because of context, by which I mean the previous actions you have taken and words you have already spoken in that relationship. The context of your factual statements may render them impotent, even destructive.

You don't have to make the same mistakes I have made. To avoid them, read the next chapter.

—————————————————————— 5

Mistakes I Have Made

"Pay to all what is owed to them: taxes to whom taxes are owed, revenue to whom revenue is owed, respect to whom respect is owed, honor to whom honor is owed." (Rom. 13:7)

"Finally, brothers, whatever is true, whatever is honorable, whatever is just, whatever is pure, whatever is lovely, whatever is commendable, if there is any excellence, if there is anything worthy of praise, think about these things." (Phil. 4:8)

The point I am making about God-centered praise of those who are not God is a point that must thread a needle having a very small eye. A single twitch to one side, and the result is man-centered, God-belittling self-esteem, missing the target entirely. A slight over-adjustment in the opposite direction and all affirmation of humans is deemed idolatrous, also missing the eye. Both errors miss the mark. This book advocates neither. I'm saying that a human can be praised and *should* be praised, but in a way that gives honor to the Maker and Sustainer of that person. When judges at the state fair award a blue ribbon for an apple pie, they commend the pie, yes, but honor for the pie's *maker* is implied, if not explicit. The pie didn't make itself. Rightly understood, the two things—honor for the pie and honor for the pie's maker—overlap and are nearly synonymous, rightly understood.

Please understand that I have no delusions about having mastered affirmation in my own behavior with polished perfection. Working on this book affords me yet another opportunity to see how far I have to go in becoming consistently refreshing to others in God-centered ways. In fact, this chapter is a catalog of mistakes I have made in the process of learning by trial and error.

While the earlier portions of this book focused on what affirmation might look like, we now address what good affirmation is not. If I am to affirm affirmation, and correct mistakes in making corrections, I must clarify what I don't mean and amplify what I do. Meanwhile, and this should not come as a complete surprise, it turns out I will affirm correction, and correct some common mistakes about affirmation.

To write a book about refreshing others while remaining an energy-draining killjoy would be hypocrisy, a serious, even heinous offense against Christ Jesus who hung bleeding to purchase my integrity. In praying for the readers of this book, I pray also for myself.

The two texts at the beginning of this chapter assert two things directly applicable to our subject. One, give honor to whom honor is owed (regardless of whether or not the person is a believer). Two, if there is anything worthy of praise, think on it, take note of it as praiseworthy, and (implicitly stated) act on that observation: that is, give praise.

What mistakes have I made in this?

Mistake: Thinking Affirmation Is Optional

Affirming others is not optional. Jesus said, "As you did *not* do it to one of the least of these, you did *not* do it to me" (Matt. 25:41). If you didn't affirm *them*, you didn't affirm *him*. I hope it doesn't peg your heresy gauge to say, "Inasmuch as you didn't praise one of the least of these, you didn't praise me." The reader might object, saying, "But isn't that idolatry?" That depends.

We make idols when we praise what God has made more than we praise God, or praise those things without regard to God. But we glorify God when we praise what he made by commending how it reflects and testifies of him. It is not dishonoring of God for us to stand in breathless awe at the foot of the Beartooth Mountains or the Colorado Rockies drinking in the subtle colors and massive scale if underneath our amazement and enjoyment is something like "look what the Creator has wrought!" If we truly marvel at things like finely spun and understated colored streaks in apple skins, the incredible intricacies of the chemical activity of subcellular physiology under the microscope, the joy and excitement of having a happy wife who says "come hither," the wonders of reproduction, or the power of water to slake thirst, float a boat, and drive a mill—and underneath we are amazed at the One who made such things and sustains them, then all the more should he be honored when we see such an unlikely thing as Christlike character in a fallen human. It's all grace. We should be amazed at the presence of the character we see, and channel that amazement toward the One who gives that quality to its undeserving host.

I am slamming the brakes on the perception that human hero worship and celebrity mindset is what I'm suggesting. But while there is unholy idolatry, there is also holy emulation.

Piper put it this way: "In spite of all the legitimate warnings against hero worship, I want to risk waving a flag for holy emulation—which includes realistic admiration. Hero worship means admiring someone for unholy reasons and seeing all he does as admirable (whether it's sin or not). Holy emulation, on the other hand, sees evidence of God's grace, and admires them for Christ's sake, and wants to learn from them and grow in them."[1]

Mistake: Thinking Affirmation Is the Chief Thing

As important as affirmation is, and even though you are reading a whole book on the subject, affirmation is not the main thing or the only thing in human relationships.

Affirmation is *a* factor, not the *only* factor in refreshing, reciprocal relationships. For example, our prayers for an individual might be infinitely more important for him than our affirmations; in fact, we might never meet the person or give him one single affirmation. I have people on my prayer list I have never met. If I never affirm them in this life, my prayers could still turn out to be crucial for them.

Christ is the main thing, and if I never affirm a person but leave him with Christ, I have done the infinitely more important thing. Meanwhile, not being the main thing does not make affirmation unimportant.

Mistake: Aiming for Greater Self-Esteem

Affirmation is *not* about building self-esteem. I am not saying that affirmed people *deserve* praise (other than affirming Christ who deserves all praise). If praise of people is taken to imply intrinsic desert, we must immediately remember there is no one good but God, as Jesus taught when he asked, "Why do you call me good?" I am arguing that the praise of character observed in people recognizes the external grace of God at work in them.

Web sites on "how to give a compliment" proliferate faster than the many rabbits that live in my neighborhood, and yet site after site promotes egotistical behavior, justifying it on the basis of "self-esteem." Instead of commending the commendable, they often commend the shallow, the transient, and even the damnable.

To commend that which God condemns is prideful and sinful, and though someone may get away with prideful schemes for a season, eventually God resists the proud: "Woe to those who call evil good and good evil, who put darkness for light and light for darkness, who put bitter for sweet and sweet for bitter!" (Isa. 5:20).

So don't commend what God condemns, but commend what God commends, especially the character of his Son. Tabloid praise of promiscuous sexiness, mail-order catalog praise of fleeting fashion finery, adulation of wicked sports "heroes," plaudits for intellectually clever and oratorically smooth sound bites made by politicians to justify corruption, condoning with smiles the outright disobedience of toddlers and calling it "cute," and affirming garden-variety sins by making excuses for them (well, I was crabby because I was tired/sick/running late—as though crabbiness were justifiable)—these commendations are not commending the commendable. To affirm such things is to belittle God and cause harm.

Generally, we don't set out to intentionally make people feel bad. We want them to feel refreshed. But it is a destructive error to temporarily refresh them by excusing their sin. Though we don't set out to make people miserable, we should not too quickly let their consciences off the hook, but let them squirm and suffer under the weight of their sin. (This is not the same as actively *seeking* ways to make people squirm.) It is not our job but the job of the gospel to remove condemnation of sin. If we confess our sins as sin, he is faithful and just to forgive. Confession, not excuse making, is required. When we excuse sin and sweep it under the rug in order to avoid bad feelings, we short-circuit the convicting work God's Spirit is doing. Rather, let us commend our sinful acquaintances when we see them soberly considering and confessing their guilt. When we recognize their discomfort in their guilt, we can commend their sensitivity as conviction of the Holy Spirit, even when it is only incremental, tiny sensitivity and not full-blown repentance just yet. We can commend in them things like alertness (to sin), attentiveness to God's promptings that there is sin in the camp and in the heart, and things like humility and contrition in confession. We can commend their truthfulness when they call sin "sin," and refuse to call it a weakness or a bad hair day or "everybody makes mistakes." We live with tension when we say things such as, we perceive "you are not far from the kingdom of God . . ." (Mark 12:34), as Jesus said to the inquiring scribe. It is possible to affirm the "not far" without implying far enough.

Western culture's emphasis on self-esteem has resulted in a yawning response to the gospel. The main problem the gospel solves is God's wrath toward sinners, but if one's inflated self-esteem is telling him he's not all that bad really, then why is God so uptight? In fact, isn't he a bit of a crab toward people who, though they may have a few flaws, are basically pretty good folks? Doesn't he love us all and have a wonderful plan for each and every life? And so a critic of this book might well ask, doesn't the practice of affirming people—especially unregenerate sinners—by affirming qualities taken by some as "goodness" seen in them harden them toward the gospel? Yes, it could. In that sense, affirmations can act like the miracles of the ten plagues directly from God's hand, hardening the hearts of Pharaohs and Pharisees. Like miracles in the eyes of Pharaohs, affirmation, especially if it isn't God-centered, can have a hardening effect.

I am arguing here that the image of God is present in all human beings, and one way that image is displayed is in the form of character qualities; but those qualities, while genuine, are echoes of someone else. The character qualities that we see in unbelievers are not intrinsic to them. Their "goodness" is not their gift to God, but God's gift to them—common grace. The character qualities they evidence are neither intrinsic to them nor salvific. We are saved by grace alone through faith alone in Christ alone on the authority of the Scriptures alone, not by developing character qualities. As sinners we must be helped to see the despicable nature of the truth-suppressing fleshly self, and recognize that character, like righteousness, is alien and comes from outside as a gift.

Consider: we don't help people see that God is already at work in them when we act as though he is not:

> For the wrath of God is revealed from heaven against all ungodliness and unrighteousness of men, who by their unrighteousness suppress the truth. For what can be known about God is plain to them, because God has shown it to them. For his invisible attributes, namely, his eternal power and divine nature, have been clearly perceived, ever since the creation of the world, in the things that have been made. So they are without excuse. (Rom. 1:18–20)

Here we see God's wrath against the suppression of truth in unrighteousness. What truth is being suppressed? It is knowledge of God's invisible attributes, clearly perceived in the things that he has made. "Made things" include human beings. And the more clearly people are helped to see his attributes in the world of nature, including people, the more they are left without excuse and shown to be helpless and desperate without the gospel. Affirming those qualities when *we* see them can help *them* see them.

Again, there is a crucial difference between self-esteem (along with its corresponding presumed innocence, resultant self-promotion, and entitlement mindset) and self-*acceptance* (which recognizes its own intrinsic bankruptcy, that someone else is in charge as the Designer, and that his design is good—to be embraced and accepted). In that sense, self-acceptance implies Designer-acceptance, the Designer being other than the self.

Self-acceptance is not complacent laziness, as though "I guess I'm good enough." Oh the dangerous fallacy and folly of concluding, "God made me this way, and therefore he doesn't want me to change." Just as he made me as a tiny zygote while not intending for me to stay that way, I was conceived in unregenerate sin, but he does not intend for me to stay that way.

Just as the huge statue in the Lincoln Memorial resembles Abraham Lincoln in some ways, but not in all ways (e.g., it is stone, not living), people, including unregenerate sinners, resemble God, but are not God; some remain dead in trespasses and sin, even while his image is reflected in them. To affirm the character of Lincoln is not statue-esteem, and to affirm the grace of God in one's character is not aiming for self-esteem.

Mistake: Confusing Glimmers of Character with Guilt Removal

Moral reform doesn't remove guilt. By recognizing and commending the image of God in people, especially unregenerate people, we dare not make (or allow our listeners to make) the mistake of thinking they can incrementally improve their character in such a way that their guilt is not damnable. We are not to be all sunlight and sparkles about the good things God has placed in them for us to see, while turning a blind eye to their real problem: the wrath of God toward unrepentant sinners. The solution is not being a better person with more character, or better family skills, or less worrying. Thinking like that is a trap. To remove guilt we don't need moral reform, but a propitiating substitute, forgiveness, and supernatural transformation, including an alien righteousness.[2] While we don't want to put performance carts (good works) before theological horses (justification by faith), horses are more likely to take carts where we want carts to go if we remember things like carrots as well as sticks. Horses move toward carrots and away from sticks. Carrots reward movement in the right direction.

Mistake: Intimidation

Speaking of the carrot and the stick, coaches who practice intimidation of their players will find the positive results of angry rants and raves short-lived and inferior to the long-term outcomes of affirming their players. I suspect that one of the reasons some coaches have resorted to tirades is because of the short-term results, but I also suspect those short-term results are followed with long-term fallout. I much prefer coaches who teach and encourage players with lots of affirmation for the good things they are doing, or even attempting to do, rather than scolding, threatening, or throwing violent hissy fits. Most players and parents prefer coaches like that, too. Affirmation when done well is no less effective at winning than intimidation. And there are benefits to affirmation in *addition* to winning (winning is not being denigrated here) that are mentioned elsewhere in this book.[3]

Hitler, Stalin, and tyrants of every description are shortsighted to think their tactics of intimidation will yield long-term fruit. Stalin turned guns on his own soldiers to keep them from retreating. Hitler's executions of any conquered leader who did not immediately show enthusiasm toward the new regime watered the growing seeds of destruction from the inside out. To this day it would be difficult to find anyone with high regard for Hitler or Stalin. Live by the sword, die by the sword. Intimidation is short-sighted.

There is a place for both the carrot and the stick. The stick is reserved for moral infractions, and should be applied with brokenness and sorrow, not anger. Generally, the carrot not only brings performance results, but improves the atmosphere. As you know, the carrot-and-stick analogy comes from the picture of a donkey driver trying to get his beast of burden to move forward by dangling a carrot from a stick just out of reach of the donkey's mouth; on occasion the donkey must actually reach the carrot and enjoy it, since promised carrots that don't often enough become real food will cease to motivate.

Mistake: Thinking All Blessings Are Affirmations

Many people who have done things like put food on the table think they have done all that's required in order to be appreciated by their beneficiaries. "I don't beat my wife, and I have provided her with a good life insurance package." But not all blessings (like food on the table and insurance and absence of beatings) affirm. Many homeless shelters and community food pantries put food on the table, and it's a blessing for the recipients and for the community, but it's not the same as affirming the diners for character.

As an action, affirmation is an individual member of a class of actions called "blessing." And Christians should be the world's best blessers, blessing people everywhere in all kinds of gutsy, generous, risk-taking, inventive, loving ways—digging wells, building clinics, teaching literacy, preaching the gospel, remaining faithful in difficult marriages, and more.

Think of financial gifts: many people have supported orphans they have never met. Geographical separation and the corresponding absence of opportunity to affirm the character of the orphan does not cancel the benefit of the material gifts. The gifts are a blessing, but not an affirmation of Christlike character.

There are many ways to bless, affirmation being only one of the ways. There are material blessings, blessings of inclusion, and blessings of forgiveness—none of which imply character in the one being blessed. Even time *away* from people can be a gift of refreshment, giving them some privacy, not wearing out your welcome, not always being underfoot.

✘ One way to bless is through hope-giving encouragement ("Hang in there, rescue is on the way!"), and one of many ways to encourage is through affirmation ("Well done! God helped you make a difference!"). ✛

Again, not all encouragements are affirmations. "Let me babysit your children for the morning," spoken to a young mother could be very encouraging indeed without necessarily saying anything positive about her character. She might be an exemplary mother or she might be on her way to jail as a serial killer. Though related, affirmation and encouragement are not the same.

Drawn as a Venn diagram, godly affirmations might be charted like this:

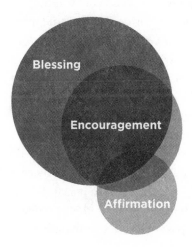

Again, not all blessings are affirmations. An inheritance received from a deceased relative might arrive as a timely blessing, but it does not necessary commend any character in the recipient, and like all blessings, it must be managed well or the blessing might end up contributing to the corruption of the recipient. God blesses *everyone* with sun and rain, and some take that blessing and grow harmful drugs. God is blessing them, not affirming them. Similarly, you might bless your family by paying the bills, but that is not the same as affirming them, and is not likely to have the same effect as affirming them.

As wonderful as blessings and encouragements are, this book is not mainly about those, but about affirmation. It's about a particular kind of blessing, a particular kind of encouragement.

Yes! Do It Like That!

Perhaps it would help to draw another distinction between encouragement and affirmation: encouragement looks forward and affirmation looks backward.

Encouragement is valid and important; however, it acts like cheerleading, spurring on the home team, psyching them up. I have chuckled at some of the curious bravado of sports teams with losing records that are so cocky in their chest-beating pre-game warm-ups and during the pregame introductions. "We're number one!" chant their cheerleaders; don't look now, but according to your win-loss record you're not number one. While it's important for coaches and parents to say things like, "Do your best, son!" and to paint a picture of a bright future that could conceivably come to pass, affirmation is different. It looks backward, confirming something that has already happened, already been observed. It commends a reality, not merely a hope. It looks at a reality that has already come into existence and says, "Yes! Do it like *that*! Do it again!" Encouragement, like cheerleading, often aims for something that has not *yet* been done (win that game, pass that test, get that job, fight that cancer, etc.)

while affirmation rewards what has *already* been demonstrated (determination in winning that game, diligence in studying for that test, perseverance in searching for that job, endurance in fighting that cancer, etc.) with the prospect that commending character in the past will foster more of it in the future.

While commending the past, affirmation is not disinterested in the future. We affirm Christlike character in the prayerful hope there will be more of it, deepened and strengthened.

The Realism of Good Affirmation

There is a distinction between affirming a solid past reality and cheering with psyched-up positive thinking. It is the difference between character already demonstrated and pie-in-the-sky positivism that presumptuously pontificates "anything you can conceive and believe, you can achieve." Baloney. We have seen a resurgence of such thinking in the wake of a recent election with pundits all over the world foolishly saying that you can be anything you want to be, like president of the United States. Well, the president's opponents—who possessed no lack of desire to be president—couldn't be anything *they* wanted to be. They wanted to be president. And neither can millions of others be president. "You can be anything you want to be" is talking nonsense, for we can desire to be a great many things we will never be. I heard a professional football athlete giving a pep talk to high schoolers telling them that if they put their minds to it, they could accomplish great things like he had. My question then is: why does he not have a Super Bowl ring? Didn't he want one?

Part of my undergraduate degree involved working in the locked psychiatric ward of a state hospital where there were folks who believed all sorts of things about themselves that they could never be. No matter how much Eddy in room 214 desires to be the grandfather of Abraham Lincoln, it ain't gonna happen, and no amount of cheerleading will get him there. As relatively harmless as his fantasy may be, it is more sensible to affirm Eddy for things like cheerful obedience when he eats his applesauce.

Mistake: Failing to Grasp the Connection between Lack of Affirmation and One's Reputation

From time to time Christians raise moral objections to issues in such ways that they become perceived as generally "anti": anti-this and anti-that, against this and against that. Such labels as "fuddy-duddies," "unloving hypocrites," "phobes," and "crabby Calvinists" are terms commonly applied. The word "puritanical" became itself a negative term in spite of the important and glorious things that Puritans *favored*. These unsavory labels stick not because Christians do not consistently advocate very good things, but because condemning, not affirming, becomes their reputation. While Christians must stand opposed to evil and must raise moral objections, when we become known for a pattern of nay-saying, we compromise—and perhaps forfeit—a hearing among our neighbors. What happens on a societal scale also happens on a personal level; just as Christians in general can take on a reputation (accurate or not), so an individual can acquire a reputation.

Yes, the world hates Jesus and will hate his followers whether they affirm or not. "For what credit is it if, when you sin and are beaten for it, you endure? But if when you do good and suffer for it you endure, this is a gracious thing in the sight of God" (1 Pet. 2:20). But it's better to be hated while affirming than hated for not affirming. Peter gives his readers a double commendation: (1) for doing good and (2) for enduring when they suffer for doing good (another Christlike character quality).

Niceness and Salvation

C. S. Lewis wrote, "When we Christians behave badly, or fail to behave well, we are making Christianity unbelievable to the outside world. The wartime posters told us that Careless Talk costs Lives. It is equally true that Careless Lives cost Talk. Our careless lives set the outer world talking; and we give them grounds for talking in a way that throws doubt on the truth of Christianity itself."

He added, "'Niceness'—wholesome, integrated personality—is an excellent thing. We must try by every medical, educational, economic, and political means in our power to produce a world where as many people as possible grow up 'nice'; just as we must try to produce a world where all have plenty to eat. But we must not suppose that even if we succeeded in making everyone nice we should have saved their souls. A world of nice people, content in their own niceness, looking no further, turned away from God, would be just as desperately in need of salvation as a miserable world—and might even be more difficult to save."[4]

Ears that really hear are a gift from God, and while there is no absolute guarantee that affirmation will win a hearing, affirmation is not a means to be overlooked in gaining a hearing. He who *wins* souls is wise. Winsomeness is a Christian virtue. Christians don't merely aim to win arguments, but to win souls. Proclamation is crucial, but so is wooing. Soul-winning is at stake.

Mistake: Overlooking the Connection between Affirmation and Soul-Winning

Who should be included as recipients of our praise? "Bless those who persecute you; bless and do not curse them" (Rom. 12:14). Of the word "bless" (*eulogize*), Matthew Henry says, "Speak well of them. If there be any thing in them that is commendable and praiseworthy, take notice of it, and mention it to their honour."[5]

Speaking the truth in love, we can affirmingly say to a hardened person something like, "I can see that you can think, and therefore I am going to give you some very difficult truth to think about." Such a direct approach affirms that God has given them capable mental faculties, while it doesn't sweep away hard news. An affirming approach does not require hiding or compromising the truth. "Repent" is a necessary message from Christians to the world (and to ourselves), but it's possible that the word "repent" (the "pill") might go down easier if it is accompanied with affirmation of the image of God in the person (the "jam"). "Repent, you repulsive, hell-bound specimen of depravity," may be exactly the truth your friend needs to hear, but he might be more likely to hear it if first he hears you say things like, "You are better than I am in many ways.[6] You don't desire to intentionally or consciously believe anything that's not true, and you prefer a future with minimal regrets. Because I assume that those important things are true about you, I invite you to think with me about something that has compellingly gripped my own attention . . ." You might then proceed to speak of whatever is true, which includes things like depravity, the wrath of God, hell, repentance, and the very bad news that makes the good news of the gospel so very good. I am not advocating a lockstep formula, a checklist, a rigid how-to formula for all gospel conversations. What I am suggesting is that a general pattern of affirming good things can keep the door open for speaking frankly about difficult and unsavory things, like damnation.

I was speaking to several hundred inmates at a correctional facility (interesting name for a facility, given our subject), and my text was Hebrews 3:12–14:

> Take care, brothers, lest there be in any of you an evil, unbelieving heart, leading you to fall away from the living God. But exhort one another every day, as long as it is called "today," that none of you may be hardened by the deceitfulness of sin. For we have come to share in Christ, if indeed we hold our original confidence firm to the end.

I wanted the inmates, who generally have pretty active hypocrisy antennae and are able to spot phonies and shams a mile away, to hear some stern warnings about evil, unbelieving hearts, falling away from the living God, being hardened, and being deceived by sin. It simply would not do to tiptoe around these exhortations—which are written for their good! So I began with the fourth warning I just listed, and spoke something like this: "If you are like me, you do not want to be snookered. You do not want to be deceived. Even if you have not been very alert or wise in the past and have been drawn into sinful schemes, the very fact that you have a desire to not be fooled the way you have been is evidence that God is at work in you. How are we, you and I, going to avoid being deceived? We would be helped if someone spoke very candidly to us, and we listened." And I went on from there. Afterward, some of the inmates (and a staff psychologist) commented to me how it was unusual for that group to let anyone speak to them so straightforwardly about being deceived. A reader might object, saying, "You appealed to their pride, not their character." Maybe. But I made it clear that they (along with all of us) have been deceived, which doesn't appeal to pride, but to humble admission.

I am trying to avoid either/or thinking, the inclination to think either a person is to be endorsed as a finished product entirely without defect, or condemned as all bad without a single feature to commend. Neither is true in this world. Beware of blanket endorsements and blanket condemnations. The situation in the real world is more complicated than that.

We must leave room in our thinking for the possibility of being pleased with someone, yet without being satisfied entirely. We commend the first faltering steps of the toddler without abandoning hope he'll someday pole-vault. We commend the first successful day of going without cigarettes while still hoping for a complete break. We commend improvement without settling for mediocrity, applauding incremental progress without confusing it with perfection. To praise someone doesn't mean we have to give up our desire that they make even greater strides. God himself treats us this way. "Good job with five talents. Now try ten. No, eleven."

Mistake: Abandoned on the Way to Hell

When I say that our failure to affirm those around us may abandon them on their hell-bent path, I am not saying that affirming them will save them any more than preaching is guaranteed to save anyone. Scripture asks how people will believe unless they hear and how will they hear unless someone preaches (Rom. 10:14). But the Bible is not saying that preaching will guarantee their salvation. For one thing, there is good preaching and there is bad preaching, and bad preaching can put obstacles (passively *leave* obstacles or actively *put* obstacles) in the way of people's "hearing" well. While not guaranteeing that preaching will save, the Bible is saying that a *lack* of preaching will unfortunately result in their *not* being saved. Salvation will not happen in the absence of preaching, but salvation is not guaranteed in the presence of preaching. Similarly, affirming people will save no one. But lack of affirmation may bring hindrances and obstacles into play, making it less likely that they will give the gospel a hearing, especially when the good news comes from someone who is predominantly bad news. Hearing is not guaranteed in the presence of affirmation, but hearing is less likely in its absence, particularly in the context of ever-present criticism.

Preaching is one of those many factors to which I allude elsewhere, factors that are ten thousand times more important than affirmation. But without our affirmation our listeners may tune out our preaching, and may have done so already. Our fine preaching, in spite of its truthfulness and biblicity and "love," may bounce off the ears of the listener. I am not limiting the power of the Holy Spirit when I talk this way. The Holy Spirit can break in on a person in the context of defective preaching (in fact, all preaching in this age is defective—there is no other kind). However, the Holy Spirit might also let the affirmation ratio play out, because God is the God not only of preaching and its effects but of other means and their effects, too.

Mistake: Confusing Affirmation with Flattery

Affirming is distinct from flattery:

> A lying tongue hates its victims, and a flattering mouth works ruin. (Prov. 26:28)

> A man who flatters his neighbor spreads a net for his feet. (Prov. 29:5)

That's the Bible, and it's echoed in secular statements like: "Flattery corrupts both the receiver and the giver"[7] and "Flattery feeds the pride of both parties."[8]

What is flattery? Like other corruptions, it starts out rooted in a good thing, but ends up putting a corrupt twist on that good thing. For example, fornication puts a corrupt twist on the God-given desire to express intimacy sexually. Gluttony puts a corrupt twist on the God-given practice of eating, which can be a wholesome interaction between stomachs and food, both given by God as good things. Gossip takes God-given things like truth and speech and puts a corrupt twist on them so that they become meddlesome and defaming. Similarly, affirmation is good, but flattery puts a corrupt twist on it.

In order to avoid folly and corruption, how shall we distinguish flattery from affirmation? While affirmation commends virtues, flattery exaggerates them, glosses over flaws, offers excessive input, and is insincere, not chiefly interested in building up the recipient in Christlikeness, but interested chiefly in obtaining some kind of direct favor. Healthy affirmation does not exaggerate or schmooze. Having affirmed, the affirmer can walk away with no expectation of receiving anything from the recipient. A good affirmer, just as the giver of a cup of cold water, looks to God for his reward. In contrast, there is a thread of seduction in flattery. The flatterer is after something from the flattered. While affirmation is a free gift with no strings attached and trusts God to bring about whatever good harvest he wishes to bring from the seed planted, flattery is a bribe, and a direct return is expected—soon.

Godly affirmation approves of Christlikeness and disapproves of anything contrary, whereas the flatterer approves anything—Christlike or not—that may achieve the desired response.

Mistake: Letting the Moment Pass

When we recognize that someone has done something commendable, we don't have to wait for him to cross our path in order to commend the commendable. While great affirmations can be made directly to the party in question, they can also be made indirectly. So affirm people behind their backs! While I have argued that one of the great benefits of affirming people to their face is that you may gain a hearing with them, gaining a hearing is not the only reason or the main reason to affirm Christlikeness. The atmosphere of a home, workplace, school, or church is uplifted by affirmations not only made directly to people, but affirmations of persons not immediately present. For example:

- "Our custodians are so attentive to detail, so willing to interrupt what they're doing to make themselves available, and so faithful to have rooms ready on time for events."
- "Wasn't Pastor's message this week faithful to the Word and encouraging to the downhearted?"

- "Did you see the paper this morning? I appreciate the courage it took those community leaders to take the action they did."
- "I think my grandfather was wise when he said . . ."
- Affirm God to others, too. "What a beautiful day! Isn't the Creator gloriously creative?" (Obviously, we can't praise God behind his back.)

Did you notice? The attentiveness, availability, faithfulness, courage, wisdom, and creativity mentioned above are Christlike character qualities. Again, by affirming in such ways behind the backs of the affirmed, we endorse the qualities—not just the persons—to which we draw attention.

At the risk of recommending something that can be abused in a manipulative way, let me quote secular writer Haim Ginott: "If you want your children to improve, let them overhear the nice things you say about them to others."[9]

Not only commend people to their faces (or in letters), but commend them behind their backs, *whether or not* the report ever gets back to them. For one thing, if you only commend people to their faces, the temptation to flattery may rise, politicizing the process, possibly contaminating it with favor-seeking or hoped-for reciprocity. For another, let God be your reward for doing your good deeds "secretly." Third, commending the qualities of persons who are absent nevertheless affirms the characteristic in focus and serves as a teachable moment for others and a reminder to yourself, holding up a commendable standard. Fourth, it makes positive use of the grapevine rather than negative gossipy use.

Affirmation Is Generally More Fitting for Individuals Than for Groups

The principle of affirmation works best with individuals, not institutions. For example, Jewish groups and genocidal anti-

Semitic groups may find humanly insurmountable obstacles to being heard by each other. Having granted such difficulties, nevertheless, such groups are made up of individuals, and individuals show increased prospects for being heard by their counterparts when they practice the power of affirmation rather than ignoring that power—if desiring to be heard is a goal.

Affirmation of the individual can be custom-tailored to his performance. On the other hand, while groups may have an average performance—"Your diligence as a sales force has resulted in a 13 percent increase in sales contacts for the company" or "You kids were very attentive in church this morning"—individuals within the group may not fit the affirmation—like the salesman who was frankly quite lazy and little Johnny who had ants in his pants. That doesn't make affirmation of groups wrong, just more ambiguous, less precise. And notice: even Christ-denying groups can unwittingly point to Jesus by doing such things as commending each other for keeping their respective end of treaties. Promise-keeping is rooted in God and should be commended wherever it breaks out.

Mistake: Failing to Give the Benefit of the Doubt

Don't know whether to affirm? Give the benefit of the doubt. Isn't that how you would like to be treated?

A word to preachers and teachers: give your congregation the benefit of the doubt that they may possess knowledge. They may know the very thing you are about to teach. Don't assume your message is the first time they have considered such things. Don't preach down to them.

On the way to becoming a certified public school teacher, I experienced several practicums, one of which was at a kindergarten where I was assigned to bring a geometry lesson adapted for that age group. I brought to class a set of large plastic three-dimensional shapes—a cone, a pyramid, a sphere, a cylinder, and so on. My aim on this day was to familiarize the kindergarteners with the cube, so holding up a bright yellow cube for all to see I asked, "Can anyone tell us what this is?" My expectation was that I might hear answers like box, square, or even the answer I was looking for: cube. But as quick as a wink, one little precocious fella matter-of-factly pronounced, "It's a parallelepiped." I was floored. He was, of course, correct, but I didn't expect such vocabulary in a kindergartener. Be careful about assuming you know something that your hearers don't. (You probably already know this.)

It's generally not considered affirming to be treated as ignorant. If that's true, what shall we do if people really are ignorant? We can say things like, "You may already know the main point of this text, and may know more about it than I do, but to ensure we all see it together, let me draw your attention to . . ."

Ask yourself, where would Christianity be today without the risky, timely, and crucially important affirmation offered by Ananias in giving the benefit of the doubt and speaking up for a notorious murderer? The ninth chapter of Acts records how Paul, now converted and marvelously transformed from the previously murderous Saul that he was, is affirmed by Ananias. It's not as though Ananias doesn't have serious reservations in his own mind. Over Ananias's earnest misgivings about Paul, the Lord says, "Go! This man is my chosen instrument . . ." (Acts 9:15). Remember, up to that point Paul has shown little fruit of repentance. But God says Paul is chosen. Chosen! What an affirmation: chosen by God! Not rejected, not abandoned, not cursed; Paul does not even encounter passive neutral indifference from God. Note that because God decisively chooses Paul *prior* to any transformation, Paul cannot boast; Ananias affirms Paul because of *God's* work.

We Christians are vulnerable to a tendency to consider unrepentant sinners as more sinful than we. But we Christians are sinners, too. Paul is chosen by God *before* he repents. But so is Ananias. Ananias is prechosen by God to be a messenger, an affirmer, before Ananias volunteers for the job.

Ananias calls Paul his brother! Do you see it? Even with the old name, the name that hearkens back to murderous persecution of the believers, Ananias affirms Saul as a brother. And before the end of the chapter, Barnabas, well-known as an encourager, will also accompany Paul (now with a new name) and defend him.

Mistake: Squandering the Hearing Once Gained

Once you have gained a hearing, say things worth hearing. Once people tune in to your radio frequency, give them something worth listening to. Point people in the direction of supremely valuing the supremely valuable, namely Christ Jesus. Many people have established very open relationships with their spouses, children, and others, yet the airwaves are filled with banality or with silence, noses buried in laptops, sportscasts, and the like.

We are called not only to avoid bad speech, but to utter good speech.

Mistake: Blindness to My Own Hypocrisy

One of the biggest stumbling blocks in relationships is Jesus' principle of the log in the eye. We so easily spot the specks in the eyes of others, but our own hypocrisy blinds us to the glaring shortcomings in our own performance. Others see our log and are turned off by our hypocrisy when we're attempting to take corrective action on their tiny little speck. It's off-putting.

I anticipate helpful criticism in the form of questions I have not anticipated or answered in this chapter. I welcome such questions, and have tried to address some in the next chapter.

6

Questions and Answers

I'm not a good affirmer. I just don't have what it takes. It doesn't fit my personality. What hope is there for me?

First answer this question: Is affirming others a good work? If it is, then plug that truth in to the following text: "And God is able to make all grace abound to you, so that having all sufficiency in all things at all times, you may abound in every good work" (2 Cor. 9:8).

Okay, you're not able. But God *is* able, and he is able to make you abound in every good work, including affirming those he has placed around you for the purpose of being refreshed by you. What hope is there for you? God.

Having received grace, "Say not you cannot gladden, elevate, and set free; that you have nothing of the grace of influence. . . ."[1]

What kind of attitude will make a person a better affirmer of others?

This is a wise question, for it goes to the heart. When it comes to affirming others well, ya gotta wanna. Generally, our failure to affirm others is not rooted in them, but in us. So ask God for personal transformation, including the development of things like greater alertness (from a heart actively on the lookout for the image of God in others), greater humility (considering others better than yourself), and greater gratefulness (appreciating how God has surrounded you with so many echoes and reflections of himself).

If I have to keep up a barrage of affirmation in order to keep correction from sabotaging my relationships, that doesn't seem like good news. It doesn't seem like gospel. It seems like the enslavement of works righteousness, which is bad news.

True, affirmation of your neighbor does not earn salvation for you. But Christ's saving you puts love in your heart and the desire to refresh and affirm your neighbor, especially when you see in him the image of Christ. Affirming others doesn't save you, but may be one kind of evidence that flows from being saved.

I've tried all this. It didn't work.

Consider the following questions.

1. If we asked the people you are trying to affirm, what would they say? Do they generally get refreshment from being around you? Would they say you are practicing affirmation as a predominant pattern in your relationship with them?
2. How long have you been at it? You may have first dug a very large hole, overspent your account, or picked a scab that needs more time and more healing salve.
3. Have you put an artificial deadline on God to act?

4. Are you doing it only if "it works," meaning that people shape up? Rather, affirm because it's right, looking to God to be your reward.

Okay, in your previous response, when I say I've tried all this, you basically respond by asking, "Did you really?" But with God as my witness, and with testimony from angels from heaven, and with the confirmation of all the eyewitnesses who know me and observe me, I really do practice a generous, happy pattern of affirmation, and yet I am not seeing improvement in one of my relationships. What then?

Like the key to your house, affirmation is key to relationships. However, as important as it is, affirmation is only one variable. You might be using your key just fine, but the lock is damaged or the dead bolt is dead or the hinges are rusted frozen or the door frame is warped or . . . The variables are many. Human relationships are complex, and God oversees all of them in all their complexities. The point of this book is to shine light on *one* of the variables—a crucial one often overlooked. Just as a door may not open for many reasons other than failure to use a key, a relationship may remain closed due to many other possible factors—demons (see Mark 9:17–29); sickness; an old, deep wound; a deep-seated neurosis.

I know some of my efforts to affirm have been hit and miss, and have not been first-class affirmations, but isn't it the thought that counts?

Yes, the thought counts; but execution counts, too, like it counts for the pitcher who didn't mean to throw the hanging fastball that the slugger belted over the fence, and like the driver who didn't mean to back over the mailbox. The affirmer who thinks his good intentions are all that count is in for a rude awakening. Practitioners had good intentions when they drained George Washington's blood, but it left him dead nonetheless. Moral parents and spouses plus good intentions can still add up to closed relationships and a roller coaster of hope one day and despair the next. Excellence and consistency matter, and lack of them hinders.

Affirmation seems so simple. What else are people attempting instead?

Many fine, intelligent, and well-intentioned people have found themselves in a relational mess—painful and puzzling, on a trajectory that does not seem hopeful. Nothing they're doing works, and God seems far off in the whole affair.

People often go down false trails, such as:

- *Prayer*, by which I mean a certain kind of praying, as though God ordains only ends and not means to ends. Yes, God can override the natural by means of the supernatural. Yes, yes, yes! By all means pray! But in addition to the supernatural he often works through the natural, and there are fundamental laws wired into human nature. And one of them is that people tend to be influenced by those who commend them. While praying for a relational breakthrough, keep on commending the commendable.

- *Counseling*, by which I mean one of the parties is sent to a counselor as though the problem is with one of the parties. But the problem is *between* the parties. I have conversed one-on-one in my office with young people who were sent by their parents, young people who were polite, respectful, and cooperative. Their problem wasn't with me; it was with their parents. Counseling "therapy" isn't what's called for, though some straightforward counsel may help, including counsel in books like this one.

- *Passivity*, by which I mean basically doing nothing, as though time alone will automatically heal all relational wounds, as though you can leave people alone and they'll come home wagging their unaffirmed tails behind them. When it comes to the affirmation ratio, doing nothing adds nothing. The overdrawn checking account needs deposits, not mere waiting for the problem to go away.

But I'm tired of affirming such unresponsive people.
Love keeps on. *Be* loving, even when others don't reciprocate. Take another glance at the benefits of affirming listed in chapter 3, and ask God to energize you for the work to which he calls us.

Do consistent patterns of active and enthusiastically heartfelt affirmations guarantee there will be no prodigals?

I know it's possible for parents to "do everything right" and still have to endure the heartbreak of a prodigal. God himself who does no wrong has endured wayward children. But I also know of parents who *claim* to have done "everything right," and yet I have observed the pattern of their relationship with their prodigals—imbalanced toward criticism and correction while nearly absent of affirmation. They have *not* done everything they could. My plea for them for the sake of their joy is to prayerfully guard against self-congratulation as though nothing more can be done.

Let us disabuse ourselves of thinking we have done everything right. There are no flawless human parents. Right off the bat we err by passing on to our children Adam's spiritual DNA. Yes, adopted children have it, too. The best of human parents may face prodigality; we all drag our far-from-finished sanctification into relationships.

How long is this going to take? I've been affirming my (spouse, teen, mother-in-law) for years, and nothing seems to be happening.

Beware of giving God deadlines. While he promises you will be rewarded for the cup of cold water you provide, he doesn't say when. The only chronology provided in Matthew 10:42, the only answer to the question "when?" is: future. Future doesn't mean never. It means not necessarily during the season of providing refreshment, or immediately thereafter, or on a timeframe of human choosing.

Some "results" of consistently affirming you will see right away, such as a heightened sensitivity to the work of God in the lives of people around you and improvement in your own behavior toward them. Other "results" may take longer, much longer.

If we already know how to affirm, and if affirming others is not difficult or overly complicated, why don't we do more of it? Why do so many relationships languish for lack of a good word?

This book is intended to reduce the quantity of languishing. Reasons affirmation doesn't happen include:

1. We don't know about the power of affirmation. We know *how* to affirm, but we don't practice affirmation as though we understand how important and effective it is.

2. We don't believe its forces are in play. We think it isn't all that powerful or important.

3. We get preoccupied and busy, passively neglecting the positive. I suspect this is a main reason why affirmation fades into the background of relationships that start out so well between well-intentioned parties.

118

4. Our focus gets hijacked, zeroing in on some desired correction, intensifying the negative. We're irked, and until we get the irritating rock out of our shoe, we aren't interested in taking any more steps toward affirmation.

5. We lack good modeling. We haven't seen it done well, and we copy the bad examples around us.

I really don't think I do that much criticizing, yet my relationship seems very strained. Am I missing something?
Perhaps. Maybe you are not correcting with scoldings or even with words, but with actions. For example, after she has adjusted the thermostat to one temperature, do you adjust it to another? The same goes for the volume dial on the car radio, etc.

I am not saying that the thermostat or car radio should not be adjusted. You could have all the best rationale for certain actions. But I want you to be aware that the other person may be taking it as correction, and therefore you may be piling it high on the correction side of the teeter-totter. The affirmation ratio is at work, even when your rationale for making the corrections you are making is completely justified. The dynamics in play don't go away just because you have taken the right position on the issue. You may be supporting the right political candidate, but removing the bumper stickers from your neighbor's car may fail to win him over, just as putting your own bumper stickers on his car may alienate rather than persuade. *LOL* - - -

Are we "Good-job!"-ing our kids to pieces?[2]
The premise of the question is an assertion by educators and child development experts that the self-esteem movement of the 1980s did kids a disservice and adults should resist overpraising. (Does your "caution antenna" perk up when the word "experts" is used? Mine does.)

Well, of course *over*praising should be resisted. That's what *over*praising is: it's too much. The fact that it is *over*praising is what puts it out of bounds. But what constitutes overpraising?

What is affirmation overload? The alarm being sounded is that if children get strokes for everything, they will come to expect praise, perhaps thinking everything they do is great. True, if they conclude that their character strengths are not a gift but up-by-the-bootstraps, self-made merit, we will contribute to the corruption of their character. We don't want to create what Lou Priolo calls "affirmation junkies" and what Joyce Meyer calls "approval addicts."

Let's go farther. To say things like "you deserve better" is to make a profound mistake. "You deserve better" is not what I mean by affirming anyone (except God himself). Godly character in people should be praised, but they cannot take credit for that character, ultimately.

Perhaps the quantity of affirmation is the problem, but I don't think so. I'm arguing here that what is out of place is the *kind* of affirmation. God-centeredness is the key. If affirmation of kids terminates on them—if *they* are great in and of themselves—then, yes, trouble is on the way. But if affirmation terminates on God who works in them to will and to do his good pleasure, then (1) let it be said that such affirmation is humbling, not puffing, and (2) affirmation that points to the attributes of God *can't* be done too much. The solution isn't to affirm less, but to affirm differently.

Dr. Ernie Swihart is concerned that if kids get kudos, it can be a recipe for needing therapy later; they will be ill-prepared to receive criticism later in life.[3] My answer: the way to prepare to receive criticism is not to subtract affirmation, but to receive criticism rightly given. Remember: the affirmation ratio is a ratio, a proportionality; correction is not removed from the picture. While Joyce Meyer is concerned about creating "approval addicts," we should admit the human race is *already* a race of approval addicts. Seeking approval is what human hearts do. We should ultimately seek approval from the right place for the right reason: from God, for imitating (living forth the life of) his Son. ✳

But if we commend unbelievers who don't grasp the Christ-centeredness of our affirmations, won't they turn the praise upon themselves and be made self-congratulating on their way to hell, in spite of our good intentions?

That's possible, in a similar way that it's possible for people to read about the unspeakable mercy and grace in Romans 1–5 and falsely conclude that we should go on sinning so that grace may abound, or falsely conclude that since the end hasn't come yet there's no need to get serious about the Bible's claims about coming judgment. There are countless other ways in which the good deeds of Christians will be interpreted as a license to sin. But the licentiousness of unbelievers won't be solved by not commending the commendable. Rather, our job remains to strive to be more and more explicit and clear in what (or who) it is we are commending. Not every passing remark can be accompanied with a full gospel explanation, but the longer we know someone and the more repeated our commendations are, the more opportunity we should seize to make clear the Christ-centeredness of our affirmations. To not do so brings into question whether we ourselves are as Christ-centered as we may think we are.

✳ The good things unregenerate people do really are good things, even if inferior to how good they would be if done consciously for the glory of God. This is one reason why I think we can and should praise young children who are not yet believers.✳

How is your position not the equivalent of straightforward behaviorism? Are you not suggesting we simply reward behavior as though people were in Skinner boxes?

While pursuing degrees in psychological fields, I was required to pass tests on Skinnerian behaviorism. B. F. Skinner was heavily influenced by the atheism of Darwin and the man-centeredness of writers like John Thorndike, so much so that his presuppositions were naturalistic, discarding all consideration of the supernatural. He called his behaviorism Radical Behaviorism. Naturalistic behaviorism gives reinforcement *all* the power. Operant conditioning is king.

I am not relegating all influence to affirmation. There is a God and he is sovereign. Darwin, Thorndike, Skinner, and others are mistaken in that respect. I am not suggesting that the people you wish to influence are cats in Thorndike's mazes or pigeons in Skinner's boxes.

Meanwhile, not everything about behaviorism is wrong, any more than Darwin's false conclusions about God mean that he didn't observe real variations among finches on the Galapagos Islands. I agree with behaviorism when it says behaviors that are rewarded tend to be repeated, and we forfeit influence if we pretend it is not so.

God is not a strict "radical behaviorist" when he teaches us that one of the explicit purposes of civil government is to affirm good behavior: "For rulers are not a terror to good conduct, but to bad. Would you have no fear of the one who is in authority? Then do what is good, and you will *receive his approval*, for he is God's servant for your good . . ." (Rom. 13:3–4). God is not dependent upon behaviorism to bring about change in people, but behaviorism is dependent upon God at every point, whether the dependence is recognized and admitted or not.

By focusing on a mechanism, namely, how failing to affirm can close down relationships and how affirmation can open up relationships, aren't you fostering a man-centered, mechanistic approach, taking God out of the picture?
Not any more than the person who writes about how hammers wielded in certain ways drive nails or bruise thumbs. The physics and mechanics of hammers and nails are designed and governed

by God. The same goes for the principles and mechanics of human nature, which he designed to operate in certain ways, tending to bring about certain effects.

I am not talking about mere pep talks, trying to psyche somebody up with feel-happy-stay-happy, you-can-do-anything cheerleading. Our aim is to build up others in Christlikeness as God gives grace, especially affirming the transforming work that God is doing in them as they abide in Christ by faith.

Isn't it oxymoronic to praise humility?

We of course face a paradox here. The most humble person to ever live pointed out his own lowliness and urged others to imitate him in it: "Take my yoke upon you, and learn from me, for I am gentle and lowly in heart, and you will find rest for your souls" (Matt. 11:29).

Jesus could say, "I'm really humble. I'm the best at it. Watch me. Then imitate my humility. It will mean a yoke for you, as it does for me." It is not oxymoronic to claim to have the world's greatest humility if the claim is true. Humility is very realistic, embracing what is. Our own humility so easily becomes contaminated with self-preoccupied pride, and then out goes whatever humility was there in the first place. Almost the moment we glimpse any shred of humility in ourselves, we are thinking not of our excellence in meeting a standard by God's grace, but of our intrinsic worthiness, and that's the death of humility. However, we can humbly spot humility in others, people whose humility is greater than our own, and point it out without ruining their humility, especially if we point it out to persons other than the humble one.

Luke records Jesus' penetrating connection in making two remarks back-to-back. First: "No one after lighting a lamp puts it in a cellar or under a basket, but on a stand, so that those who enter may see the light" (Luke 11:33). So lamps are to be put on lampstands in order to help others see. On the heels of that statement comes this: "Your eye is the lamp of your body . . ." (v. 34).

In other words, your eye—when revealing what it sees—helps others see. Translation: when you see truth, don't hide it. In the context of this book, when you see evidence of God's work in a life, help others see it, too. In his record of the Sermon on the Mount, though Matthew separates Jesus' teaching about the lamp from his teaching about the light of the body by fifty-three verses, we see this: "In the same way [as on a lampstand], let your light shine before others, so that they may see your good works and give glory to your Father who is in heaven" (Matt. 5:16).

What good works will they see? Well, no good works (except secret ones) are excluded, but it's possible that the good work in mind is "light shining." You shine light, and others get the benefit of that light. Specifically, with your eye—which is the lamp—you see the glory of God in his workmanship, and when you point out his work, others see it too, joining in the giving of glory. When we point out the work of God in the lives of others, he gets glory, others start seeing what they may have overlooked, and our eye fulfills its role as a lamp.[4]

How is it possible to have and to express longings for family members (to make changes) without the expression of those longings coming across as indictment or disappointment that crushes the relationship?[5]

This is a very good question, for most of us have experienced that kind of crushing disappointment. The argument in this book is that while ratio is *one* factor, an important one, there are other factors, such as prayer (asking God to work in you and in them), timing (not engaging in disputes when angry or sick or weary at the end of the day), humility and an attitude of brokenness (instead of arrogance or critically lording it over others), and more—each of which is worthy of its own book.

But the factor I am underscoring in this book is ratio or pro-portionality. In fact, I am arguing that God may allow all the other factors, including prayer, to be held hostage by failure to practice affirmation. → Am I not Affirming Kari & Kyle enough ??

Our love for others will necessarily cause us to long for them to make improvements in their habits, gains in their sanctifi-cation. But if their impression of our attitude toward them is mainly that of longing for change, and not mainly thanks to God, the next suggestion or criticism coming from us may feel to them like piling on. ✳ Johnny ??

So when desiring to express longings without coming across as indicting, work overtime at affirmation first. As much at it lies with you, ensure that the context or backdrop of expressed shortcomings is an environment of affirmation and approval.

Also, choose carefully which longings rise to the level of being expressed. Not all desired improvements are worth the attention and energy it will take to deal with them.

Can prayer be held hostage by lack of affirmation?
Yes. Here's a specific instance:

> Likewise, husbands, live with your wives in an understanding way, *showing honor* to the woman as the weaker vessel, since they are heirs with you of the grace of life, *so that your prayers may not be hindered.* (1 Pet. 3:7)

Answered prayer is another undeserved mercy from God. It's quite conceivable that he won't answer my prayer for a healed toe before I lift the anvil off it or for weight loss while I chow down a box of Hostess cupcakes. In the same way, he may not grant my request to cause the other person to listen to me with an open mind as long as I keep slamming the relational door with my gusts of critical wind.

125

How can we discern the difference between words that are simply objective in criticism and words that are downright demeaning?

Your discernment in asking such a perceptive question leads me to suspect that you are well on your way to healthy application of the distinction.

Correction must be performed—love must do it—but it is risky business. There are hope-giving ways to make suggestions for improvement, and there are condemning ways. Condemnation rejects the whole person along with the behavior. Condemnation writes him off as hopeless. "You jerk," is a generalization about the whole person, and does not make distinctions between strengths and weaknesses. "I have made the same mistake myself," said in the right tone of voice and with the right look on the face can be a helpful preamble to a correction that is not condemning of the person. Before criticizing and while criticizing, hold onto the good: "test everything; hold fast what is good" (1 Thess. 5:21).

Criticism aimed at helping a person succeed in becoming more like Christ is different from merely expressing irritation at someone who has disappointed or inconvenienced you, or embarrassed your pride. "I've had it with you" is a sweeping condemnation of the whole person, not just a desire for improvement in one area.

Corrections can be made without becoming put-downs. Without a steady diet of affirmations, however, corrections can be *taken* as put-downs, even if they were not meant as put-downs.

When discussing 2 Timothy 1:16–18 (in chap. 2), you said that if we want mercy from God we should refresh others. Are you saying that mercy is earned?

No. That would make mercy something other than what it is. Mercy is never earned. I am no more saying that mercy is earned than Jesus was saying it is earned when he taught, "Blessed are the merciful, for they shall receive mercy" (Matt. 5:7). Except in God's case, the showing of mercy is evidence of having received it. Conversely, a person who does not show mercy demonstrates that he is not responding to the great mercy of God, and is in peril of damnation. "For judgment is without mercy to one who has shown no mercy . . ." (James 2:13). Perhaps it would help to think of it in reverse order: a person receives mercy on the day of judgment. Prior to that day, the person at various points in his life demonstrates mercy toward others. And prior to that, the mercy of the Lord reaches him, transforming him, so that he desires to be merciful to his neighbor. God acts first. The mercy a man shows is caroming mercy he first received from God, unearned and undeserved.

What's the matter with those people who don't affirm me? When is it my turn to be affirmed?

Beware seeking the praise of man. People ask this question as though it's their turn to be affirmed, and they're not about to do any more affirming of others until they see more of it coming in their direction: "Therefore you have no excuse, O man, every one of you who judges. For in passing judgment on another you condemn yourself, because you, the judge, practice the very same things" (Rom. 2:1).

Always model what it is you want from others. If you desire affirmation, model it.

What should a person do when he receives affirmation? Am I stealing honor from God when I receive affirmation?

"The crucible is for silver, and the furnace is for gold, and a man is tested by his praise" (Prov. 27:21). Praise is a test—of humility, of honesty, of God-centeredness. Deflect the praise to those who contributed to your success, especially God. Corrie ten Boom said that when people would honor her, she knew that God was really the one who deserved all the glory and credit, so

127

she would imagine each honor as a huge bouquet of roses. She would picture herself taking in their scent and savoring it for a moment before handing it up to him, the rightful recipient. Smell the roses and hand them up.[6]

Receive praise as an advance deposit on the "well done" eventually coming from God himself.

Is this business of affirmation relevant to formal affirmations, such as creeds and affirmations of faith?

A formal affirmation of faith or doctrinal statement serves important functions: correcting error, clarifying with precision what it is that we believe and what we deny, unifying those who embrace its content, and helping preserve individuals and institutions against cultural drift. Affirmations, formal and otherwise, are strengthened and clarified by denials, because love requires both approval of good things and disapproval of destructive things. Denials are important to affirmations, because otherwise, in our culture of obfuscation and Alice in Wonderland usage of words ("'When *I* use a word,' Humpty Dumpty said in a rather scornful tone, 'it means just what I choose it to mean—neither more nor less.'"[7]), speech can come to mean almost anything, like head-shakingly oxymoronic statements such as "safe abortions."

Unfortunately, there are people who upon reading a formal affirmation of faith will say something like, "I guess I can affirm that," by which they mean they can tolerate it, if they can be permitted to redefine some of the terms to mean what they would prefer the terms to mean, in opposition to what the authors meant. That kind of affirmation is wrong-headed and dangerous, because institutions and individuals who are swayed by such slippery use of language jettison meaning and resort to language only for its short-term usefulness, discarding the formal affirmation if it's not immediately useful.

If I want Satan to listen to me when I wish he would leave me alone, should I affirm him in order to get him to listen to me?

No, I don't encourage affirming Satan; I don't even encourage speaking to him at all. Though the Bible teaches that he was formerly an archangel and is able to appear as an angel of light, getting into a conversation with Satan is a very dangerous thing for a mere mortal. I don't want him talking to me, and I don't talk to him. I don't command him to get behind me, or leave. I don't speak to him at all. Instead, I speak to God *about* him, asking God to send him and his demons wherever Jesus would send them. I suggest talking to God (about Satan), and letting God talk to Satan. ✳ This is EYE opening!!

Why bother to affirm and refresh somebody who's just going to end up in hell?

First, we are gracious to all because God is: "But I say to you, Love your enemies and pray for those who persecute you, *so that* you may be sons of your Father who is in heaven. *For* he makes his sun rise on the evil *and* on the good, and sends rain on the just *and* on the unjust" (Matt. 5:44–45).

Christians bless believers and unbelievers alike, in the image of their Father who leads the way in refreshing evil people every day.

Second, it is not our business to separate wheat from tares:

He put another parable before them, saying, "The kingdom of heaven may be compared to a man who sowed good seed in his field, but while his men were sleeping, his enemy came and sowed weeds among the wheat and went away. So when the plants came up and bore grain, then the weeds appeared also. And the servants of the master of the house came and said to him, 'Master, did you not sow good seed in your field? How then does it have weeds?' He said to them, 'An enemy has done this.' So the servants said to him, 'Then do you want us to go and

129

gather them?' But he said, 'No, lest in gathering the weeds you root up the wheat along with them. *Let both grow together until the harvest*, and at harvest time I will tell the reapers, Gather the weeds first and bind them in bundles to be burned, but gather the wheat into my barn.'" (Matt. 13:24–30)

Who knows whether the unregenerate person might yet be converted?

Third, it's true that God uses pain and affliction to awaken the sinner from his rebellious ways: "Before I was afflicted I went astray, but now I keep your word" (Ps. 119:67). But it's also true that God uses kindness to bring about repentance: "Or do you presume on the riches of his kindness and forbearance and patience, not knowing that God's kindness is meant to lead you to repentance?" (Rom. 2:4). God's repentance-bringing kindness might be conveyed through your mouth, your affirming bent.

By saying that unbelievers can demonstrate character, aren't you getting the sanctification cart before the justification horse? Don't you have ordo salutis *out of whack? Are you saying a person can become righteous before salvation?*
None is righteous but God. No one but God can produce the righteousness God's righteousness requires. But before a person comes to saving faith, he might produce works we could call "good" in the common grace God supplies. We see this clearly in small children who learn to obey, to share toys, to help with chores—prior to trusting Jesus for salvation. So an unsaved person can produce good deeds, though none that merit salvation.

Couldn't unscrupulous persons use the principle that people tend to be influenced by those who praise them for corrupt purposes?
Yes and no. Yes, they may be making gifts of Trojan horses, the well-known strategy of the Greeks to enter the city of Troy by

concealing soldiers inside a huge figure of a horse, a deception. Large gifts can have the utilitarian effect that large gifts can have, and praise can have the corrupting effect that praise can have. That's the yes part of my answer. But, no, unscrupulous people are not likely to encourage Christlikeness over the long haul, and this book takes pains to caution the reader that not any old praise will do. We are aiming to refresh our neighbor for his sanctification, not his ruination. And God is judge.

Jesus had just taught on the subject of hypocrisy when he added this:

> For no good tree bears bad fruit, nor again does a bad tree bear good fruit, for each tree is known by its own fruit. For figs are not gathered from thornbushes, nor are grapes picked from a bramble bush. The good person out of the good treasure of his heart produces good, and the evil person out of his evil treasure produces evil, for out of the abundance of the heart his mouth speaks.
>
> Why do you call me "Lord, Lord," and not do what I tell you? Everyone who comes to me and hears my words and does them, I will show you what he is like: he is like a man building a house, who dug deep and laid the foundation on the rock. And when a flood arose, the stream broke against that house and could not shake it, because it had been well built. But the one who hears and does not do them is like a man who built a house on the ground without a foundation. When the stream broke against it, immediately it fell, and the ruin of that house was great. (Luke 6:43–49)

You cannot tack fruit onto a tree and suddenly have a fruit tree, any more than you can duct tape apples on a telephone pole and suddenly make an apple tree. Jesus' point is that the fruit is derived from the nature of the tree. Similarly, deeds flow out of a nature, out of a heart. Bad deeds flow from a corrupt heart, and good deeds from a transformed one. Speech is a deed. Speech comes from somewhere, namely, the nature of the speaker. Claiming Jesus as Lord simply by speaking the word "Lord" no more makes a person a believer than calling a judge "Your Honor" makes the person intrinsically honorable. True evidence of Christian faith is consistent obedience to Jesus' teaching: "Everyone who comes to me and hears my words and does them. . . ." Hypocrisy will not stand ultimately. Good deeds not done from the heart will be destroyed like houses built on shifting foundations.

What is affirmation? Can you give us a helpful definition?

Affirmation is truthfully declaring by complimentary word or action the goodness of something. Good affirmation attests, certifies, or confirms that which honors God, that which is morally upright.

7

Sightings of Jesus

Having already warned against works righteousness and cookbook checklists for outward righteousness versus an inwardly transformed life imaging forth Christ, my aim in this chapter is to show how to refresh people with affirmations that are explicitly Christ-honoring. Affirmations of Christlikeness are more precise and upbuilding than ubiquitous smiley faces. Though passing out smiley-face stickers may be better than nothing, smiley-face stickers are vague and correspondingly weak. (What are they smiling about? Depending upon the answer, it may or may not be wise to smile with them.)

I agree with Lou Priolo, who says, "Demonstrate your high estimation of others by commending them for those qualities that are biblically worthy of praise."[1] That which is most biblically worthy of praise is God himself, especially God revealed in his preeminent Son whose Spirit is at work in people.

Remember this basic assumption: if anyone does anything that pleases God, it happens because God is already at work in that person: "For it is God who works in you, both to will and to work for his good pleasure" (Phil. 2:13).

God's good pleasure centers around his Son and our worship of his Son, by imitating him: "He was still speaking when, behold, a bright cloud overshadowed them, and a voice from the cloud said, 'This is my beloved Son, with whom I am well pleased; listen to him'" (Matt. 17:5).

Listen to Jesus. What does he say? "Truly, truly, I say to you, whoever believes in me will also do the works that I do . . ." (John 14:12).

Imitating Jesus pleases God, assuming that the imitation stems from a reproduction of the life of Christ being imaged forth from the transformed one in whom he resides by faith. I am not saying that imitating Jesus pleases God when it comes from outward checklists maintained in mere human effort. That's death and deadly.

How then can we justify commending nonbelievers? One answer is to think of the way in which parents commend their small children for doing good even before those children come to faith in Christ Jesus. We hope and pray that later those deeds will be filled up with grace and belief.

It bears repeating that I am not primarily interested in generic, vanilla, fuzzy, imprecise, and dubious compliments with approval of something vague. Get specific. "Nice job"—what exactly was nice about it? "Gnarly, dude"—what aspects were so gnarly? I'm often guilty of this next one: "Remarkable"—just what is it that is so remarkable? *Remark* about it!

I desire for us to see and affirm the work of God in persons as evidenced by sightings of the character of his well-pleasing Son manifest in them. When I say, "commend the commendable," the "commendable" to which I am referring is primarily and fundamentally the character of Jesus. Everything commendable is rooted in him. All good, beauty, and excellence find their source in him and reflect him.

While it's fine to cheer on my grandson, as he toddles his first steps, saying, "Good job, Taylor!" I'm aiming for much more precise and Christ-honoring affirmations. Even though Taylor doesn't understand, onlookers do understand when I congratulate him in such ways as, "Wow! Taylor, God is really helping you develop and you are not wasting the opportunity to use the legs he has given you!" God gets the honor for the development, for the legs, and even for Taylor's enthusiasm for walking and stewardship of his developing legs. I am commending not just walking, but attitude. Taylor can discern that I am affirming him. It's not all about Taylor, but about God at work in Taylor. He'll understand more as he matures.

In order to commend the qualities of Jesus being reproduced in the lives of others, it is crucial to know the Bible, the only eyewitness account we have of Jesus' life, the only authoritative divine revelation of his life, his teachings, and his ways. To spot and affirm Christlike characteristics in people and to spot the mind and Spirit of Christ being imaged forth requires us to be familiar with that mind and that Spirit through his revealed Word, the Bible. We have no license to invent Jesus.

What is a *Christlike* characteristic? A Christlike characteristic is a marked pattern of behavior indicative of the work of God (grace). A commendable characteristic can be present in unbelievers, though without faith that characteristic will eventually atrophy. In believers, growth in character is indicative of a fruitful heart abiding in the Vine and reproducing traits and qualities derived from the Source.

Accordingly, Christlikeness is not a simple roster of attributes to mimic or a checklist of actions to reproduce in human strength, even though we can affirm our children as they make incremental progress in such things as patience, kindness, responsibility, endurance, truthfulness, and so on. Rather, true Christlike character is the outworking of the life of Christ himself, as a person abides in him by faith. It is true life, not merely a lifestyle. If the life of Christ's Spirit is not coursing through the person, aiming for true Christlikeness will remain a deeply flawed effort to pursue "works righteousness," eventually damning that person in his truth-suppressing self-righteousness.

Just as a living rabbit is more than merely an assembly of its parts, Christlikeness is more than a compilation of attributes, components, earmarks, capacities, or distinguishing features. Nevertheless, just as a living rabbit can be examined in its various parts, Christlikeness can be held up to the light to have its various facets sparkle with brilliance. Hair does not make a hare, but we can plainly observe that a healthy hare has hair. Similarly, things like compassion and courage do not make one a Christian, but if one is a Christian (supernaturally newly birthed and treasuring Christ above all), things like compassion and courage will sprout and grow. With rabbits we can look for mammalian hair and with transformed people we can look for compassion and courage. We can foster the growth of fur on the rabbit by paying attention to what fosters healthy fur and feeding the bunny well. Similarly, we can foster Christlikeness in the Christian by focusing on it and feeding him a diet of soul food that nourishes it, including affirmation.

It is important to remember that in those who love him, God is working all events and circumstances toward one thing: Christlikeness. "And we know that for those who love God *all things* work together for good, for those who are called according to his purpose. For those whom he foreknew he also predestined *to be conformed to the image of his Son*, in order that he might be the firstborn among many brothers" (Rom. 8:28–29). So, we should be on the lookout for such conforming work underway in all circumstances.

Christlike Qualities

What follows is only a sampling of the scores of Christlike qualities that we should be looking for and affirming in the lives of those around us, for Christ's glory and for their refreshment. We could catalog numerous such characteristics, but the aim here is not an exhaustive catalog, but a few examples of Jesus at work in those around us, in the hopes that readers will go on their own hunting expeditions, seeking the evidence of God's handiwork in people, sightings of Jesus.

Truthfulness. Jesus is the faithful witness (Rev. 1:5), the most truthful being in existence, the One for whom it is impossible to lie. Everything Jesus says and does corresponds with reality, and he defrauds no one. So commend truth-telling, especially when truth is spoken in love. Applaud those who make observations that accord with reality. It is not hard to say, "Good point."

Numerous mothers of young children have asked me how to foster honesty in their small children. First, model it. Second, when you spot it, affirm it—especially when honesty costs something, as in confession. When a child confesses something—perhaps he broke something—the first thing to do, before correcting the mischief, is to commend the honesty. Make a big deal out of the trustworthiness of honest people, how confidence in them grows as they make a pattern of telling the truth and how much courage it takes to tell the truth when there are consequences. If there must be consequences for misbehavior, deal with the consequences *after* first celebrating and cementing the honesty.

Obedience. Jesus is the most obedient human being ever to live, having never once disobeyed the Father in thought, word, or deed. It is astonishing that Jesus had to learn—learn!—obedience through suffering (Heb. 5:8).

It is the prospect of suffering that makes obedience difficult. If obedience were never inconvenient, never painful, never

137

Christian mocks

costly, then it would be easy. All the more reason we should give approval of it. It's hard.

The best obedience isn't reluctant resignation or acquiescence, but creative cooperation with authorities (such as parents, employers, and church elders), seeking to help them succeed in carrying out their God-given responsibilities.

Some of the most stubborn and willful rebels can be influenced, even won over, by means of honest affirmation coupled with God's grace. There is a tendency for all who are in positions of authority to simply expect obedience as an entitlement, without thanking the obedient for their cooperation. I'm saying it's good, healthy, helpful, and wise to say things like, "Thanks for picking up your things when Grandpa asks you; good job!" "Dear teenage daughter, you inspire your dad's confidence in you when you come home before curfew just as you said you would. Your cooperation is appreciated and it shows that you are developing great trustworthiness." "I understand that you have an imperfect supervisor (me) who will from time to time demonstrate his imperfection, and I have no doubt that some of you could do my supervising job better than I do, and when you become supervisor you can institute the changes that you think would be wise and helpful to make. But for the time being I just want to say that I appreciate the way you have been cooperating with the (paperwork/dress code/schedule changes/parking lot paving mess, etc.)."

Forgiveness. Jesus is the most forgiving person in existence, for he extends mercy to every sinner who confesses his sinfulness to God and trusts Jesus to pay the penalty for his God-belittling indifference and rebellion. Such forgiveness is fundamental to loving relationships, for as Jesus taught, "he who is forgiven little, loves little" (Luke 7:47).

Forgiveness is not a matter of claiming it was no big deal; if it were no big deal, it wouldn't need forgiving. Things that need forgiving are things that got Jesus killed, all of them and each of them. Offenses ruin relationships, giving rise to bitterness, vengeance, and hardened hearts.

So when you see someone give another person a second chance, commend it. When you see someone investing in a per-son who wronged him, applaud it. When you see people speaking well of those who hurt them, affirm that kind of attitude.

Alertness. No one is more alert than Jesus, being aware of what's going on and initiating all the right responses to each event and each person in each and every instance. After all, he is holding the entire created universe together at every moment.

He repeatedly cautioned his followers to stay awake, to be watchful, and to be ready. So, when you spot someone demonstrating alertness, he is echoing—however faintly or explicitly—the alertness of the One who is most alert. We should commend alertness and watchfulness in children who are learning to cross the street or handle sharp kitchen utensils, teenagers learning to drive, deacons who proactively get involved before problems get bigger, folks who pray and fast all night, and many others. Further, commending the alert may refresh them and extend their alertness.

Hospitality. Jesus is the prince of hospitality, having gone to prepare dwelling places for every believer. He shares everything he has, holding no spiritual blessing back for himself.

To cheerfully share what one has with those whom God brings into one's life requires confidence that God will yet provide everything needed for one's own good. So to commend hospitality implies commendation of contentment, too. From the toddler who offers Grandpa a lick of his cone, to the family who takes in an orphan, there are myriad sightings of hospitality to be affirmed.

Diligence. No one surpasses Jesus in applying all his energies—every last drop—to accomplish what the Father has given him to do.

Earnest, focused effort is evidence of enabling grace. Though the laborer deserves his wages for laboring, and though he will be compensated by his wages, he will be *refreshed* by appreciation and affirmation of his diligence. Unappreciated effort can be corrupted into laziness very easily.

Initiative. Jesus acts. He does not wait to be cajoled, recruited, or talked into doing what needs to be done.

Those who recognize and do what needs to be done are energized when affirmed for doing so. Be on the lookout for people who don't wait to be asked before they volunteer for that organization, grab the other end of the table, pick up the room after the meeting, offer an idea *along with* their time and energy to carry it out, push that car out of a snowbank, watch the baby for an afternoon while mommy gets a much-needed nap, and so on.

Dependability. Nobody is more dependable than Jesus, for all the promises of God are "yes" and "amen" in him, completely fulfilled (see 2 Cor. 1:20).

Dependability is promoted in a community when we praise people who do everything from showing up at meetings on time to paying tithes to their church to keeping their wedding vows decade upon decade.

This chapter has briefly shown how we can be on the lookout for only eight of the scores of Christlike qualities that can be identified and affirmed to honor the One who is the source of those qualities, to shine light on the qualities so that they are recognized, and to refresh those who replicate such qualities in the life and strength Christ supplies. The same discussion

140

could be had regarding love, joy, peace, patience, faithfulness, gentleness, self-control, orderliness, reverence, sensitivity, sincerity, generosity, justice, courage, kindness, creativity, and many more Christlike characteristics. Christ Jesus is perfect in all of them, and we are wise to do everything we can in the strength he supplies to replicate such qualities in our own lives, while encouraging and affirming them in the lives of others.

A Word about Balance

The Christlike qualities above are magnificent and worth emulating. But they do not stand alone as islands.

For example, as important as truthfulness is, it doesn't stand alone. It is balanced by other qualities. I am *not* saying that truthfulness is balanced by lies. I am saying that truthfulness is balanced by things like discretion. Not everything that is true should be spoken. Consider this: though God ordained everything that happens in the marriage bed, not all of it needs to be spoken even if true. The same goes for combinations to locks, passwords to computers, entries in personal checkbooks, and what goes on in the bathroom. Just because it's all true doesn't mean it all needs to be spoken. That's the sense in which truthfulness is balanced with things like discretion. Jesus spoke in parables, parables which are simultaneously true and mysterious.

Brutality Truth without love can be very harsh. On the other hand, love without truth is sentimentality. Obedience without discretion and courage to obey God first could result in the foolishness of drinking Kool-Aid in the jungle. All Christlike character qualities work together, not in isolation.

It takes wisdom to balance the character qualities of Christ who exercised them all in perfect balance. So wisdom is yet another Christlike quality to affirm when you see it in people.

Balance is also needed in mixing correction with affirmation, and we take up that challenge in the next chapter.

8

Mixing Correction
with Affirmation

Love must correct.

Lloyd John Ogilvie writes, "Affirmation of people does not have to mean advocacy for their wrongful lifestyle or behavior." Affirmation labors to earn a platform from which to challenge wrongful lifestyles and be heard in doing so. "The Holy Spirit does not counsel us to have a flabby, indulgent attitude. Nor does he encourage us to buy into our age of appeasement and tolerance where everything is relative and there are no absolutes. However, the Holy Spirit shows us that any judgment of people's infractions of these absolutes must be done with indefatigable love and willingness to help them."[1]

Correcting well deserves its own book. But affirmation, not correction, is the emphasis of *this* book. So instead of making a robust case for correcting well, this chapter simply warns against a few ways we tend to correct poorly, ways that may undo the good being accomplished by our affirmations.

Even if we:

- are right, not wrong,
- possess the jurisdiction, the right, even the responsibility to say something,
- apply wise and loving rationale,
- have good motives,
- love the person deeply,
- have exactly the right wording, and
- have exactly the right tone of voice,

all those things won't matter in our relationships if we have squandered a hearing, if we have alienated our listeners, if we have turned them off. It doesn't matter what perfect programs we are broadcasting over our radio channel if they're not tuned in.

One reason for rebellious kids and broken marriages is that we have homes where seldom is heard an encouraging word. Without encouraging words, the kids and spouse won't be built up and tuned in.

Even if a person understands the psychology of human development, the theology of man and sin, the best child-rearing practices, and the difference between right from wrong, the people around him are likely to stop *hearing* him over time if he doesn't practice affirmation toward them. When overwhelmed by correctives, insufficient affirmation can leave your influence held hostage.

Love must correct. But we need to heed a few cautions.

1. Speak the truth in love (Eph. 4:15). Behave in such a consistently affirming way that when correction must be made, there is no mistake in the recipient's mind

that you are for him and not against him. Yes, speak the truth. But in love, the kind of love that is expressed in ways so that it is understood by the other as love.

2. Permeate not only your *words* of truth with love, but your actions. Your actions must be consistent with your verbalizations. It will not do to make claims of affirmation while continuing to do what wounds and alienates the other person. You're already thinking it, so I'll say it: actions speak louder than words. And while understanding that actions speak louder than words, don't make the mistake of thinking that words add nothing to actions.

3. Even when speaking the truth in love, speak precisely, aiming to commend the commendable. For example, when observing improvement in someone, to say, "You're not as lousy and worthless as you used to be," may be true, but it may not seem very commendatory and refreshing to the hearer. Rather than focusing on the decrease in failure, consider commending some specific behavior to be encouraged, some positive attitude. I suppose burglars in jail could be commended for burglarizing less now that they're in jail, but how much better to commend a former burglar for doing something positive, like laboring, making restitution, or giving generously.

In the same way, double meanings are self-defeating. "It's a good thing I love idiots." Well, yes, that would be a good thing, but it may not endear you to me. And meanwhile, you have not commended anything commendable in the other person. You have boasted about your own "love." God gets no honor from your calling me an idiot.

Praise isn't only for those who are better than others. Praise is entirely fitting when progress takes place, even

145

if the performance is worse than all the others'. Athletes in the Special Olympics are given awards not just for outdoing others, but for showing determination and numerous other character qualities that even children can demonstrate.

Word selection matters. "The right word is like a drug," says Amanda Knoke.[2] She means that it diminishes pain and fosters health: "Let your speech always be gracious, seasoned with salt, so that you may know how you ought to answer each person" (Col. 4:6).

In correcting, ask: how can this correction give grace? "Let no corrupting talk come out of your mouths, *but only such as is good for building up*, as fits the occasion, that it may give grace to those who hear" (Eph. 4:29).

4. See through the other person's ears. Just because we criticize somebody doesn't mean we're showing disrespect; but if criticism continues to be the pattern from us, the fact that we don't mean it as disrespect doesn't mean it won't be *taken* as disrespect and *felt* as disrespect and hinder our relationship with that person just as disrespect would. ✱

✱ 5. Tone of voice is a sweetener or killer. Take your pick. (See appendix 2, a letter to a mother asking about the tone of voice in her home.) Tone of voice can undercut affirmations being verbalized, canceling them. Tuning you out is not necessarily conscious or intentional on the part of others.

Be alert for unintended put-downs: constant chipping, nit-picking, implying nothing's ever good enough, etc. Such negativity contradicts a believer's effort to be a testimony to unbelievers. Put-downs are off-putting to the one being put down and to onlookers as well.

146

6. Check your motives for correcting. When you correct, whose agenda are you following? Are your corrections driven by your own preferences, your own disappointments and frustrations? Or are your corrections driven by what God desires for each person? Would other godly people confirm the God-centeredness of your corrections and the authenticity of the love that is motivating you?

7. Listen before leaping. Be swift to hear, slow to speak. Listening affirms the person to whom we wish to speak, the person we want to have heard *us*. Not only that, but our active, patient listening models what we want him or her to do.

8. Be careful what you affirm. You may get more of it. Just as there are superior ways of correcting, there are superior ways of affirming.

   If we affirm trendy clothing, we may get more shallow trendiness.

   If we affirm accessories, we may get an emphasis on accessorizing.

   If we affirm only winning, we may get an increase in unscrupulous win-at-any-cost attitudes and behaviors.

   If we affirm things like Scripture memory and serving others less than we affirm dance lessons or soccer performance, we may discover a corresponding set of values and priorities developing in the life of the affirmed.

Oh, the mercy of God shown to those who are about to give up on ever restoring a relationship, and then it happens: they discover the power of affirmation.

9

100 Affirmation Ideas for Those Who Feel Stuck

Whether you are stuck because the one you wish to affirm is a difficult person (a separate chapter could be written called "Ways to Affirm *Difficult* People"), or because you have run out of ideas, or you have fallen into a rut, wearing out the same old affirmations, this chapter is for you.

Words matter. As soon as God created mankind, he engaged him verbally. Merely speaking with (not at) people can affirm their existence. You talk to me; therefore, in a sense, I am. Simply greeting someone who walks through a room can be affirming to the individual and uplifting to everyone in the environment.

God designed words to be so powerful that speech brought creation into being: "*By the word* of the LORD the heavens were made, and by the breath of his mouth all their host" (Ps. 33:6); "By faith we understand that *the universe was created by the word* of God, so that what is seen was not made out of things that are visible" (Heb. 11:3).

And like water to a dry garden, speech has the strange and wonderful power to penetrate the soul and bring refreshment. A good word overcomes anxiety: "Anxiety in a man's heart weighs him down, but a good word makes him glad" (Prov. 12:25).

"It would seem as if very few of us give this power of kind words the consideration which is due to it."[1] First Thessalonians 4:18 says, "Therefore encourage one another *with these words.*"

We dare not take the seriousness of our speech for granted, for Jesus says that even our justification or condemnation is at stake: "I tell you, on the day of judgment people will give account for every careless word they speak, for *by your words* you will be justified, and *by your words* you will be condemned" (Matt. 12:36–37).

Words have been endowed with the capacity to change lives, to bring arresting transformation. They have the curious and uncanny power to make living things die or bring dead things to life: "Death and life are in the power of the tongue, and those who love it will eat its fruits" (Prov. 18:21).

Do you see? There is a fruit to be harvested as a consequence of how we speak. God has designed speech in accordance with the law of the harvest: reaping follows planting, the crop matches the seed sown, and the harvest is greater in quantity than the amount sown. Harvests and seeds: ends and means to ends. That's the way God designed it. Speech yields reactions; therefore, "Whoever keeps his mouth and his tongue keeps himself out of trouble" (Prov. 21:23).

Let me be the first to say that my own unruly tongue has triggered many an unfortunate reaction. I am writing this book to myself, because I fall so far short of being the kind of affirmer that would please God and refresh others around me.

Practicing the following list will not give you the life of Christ or transform your heart so that you want to be an affirming person. But if you have the life of Christ in you and you want to be a blessing to others, the following list might assist you to that end. A list will not save you, but if you are saved, you might find a list useful.

100 Ideas for Those Who Feel Stuck

1. Loan a young person your keys. Or give him his own key.

2. At a committee or board meeting, before moving on to the next agenda item, stop to commend those who worked on the previous item.

3. Write a personal letter or note card that an employee can take home or put in a personnel file. Keep a supply of such blank note cards in your desk for just such a purpose. E-mails will do, but they are less likely to be pinned up on workspace walls or put in a portfolio.

Good idea!

4. Commend the wisdom and helpfulness of a suggestion somebody has made, especially when the suggester has offered to be a part of a solution to a problem.

5. Explain that what inspired you to do some good thing was the other person's example. "I brought coffee cake for the office because I see how much the staff enjoys it when *you* consistently do thoughtful things."

6. Don't talk down to people; talk up to them. Consider them better than you. "Do nothing from rivalry or conceit, but in humility count others more significant than yourselves" (Phil. 2:3). "You probably already know this, but. . . ."

7. Just as God decisively chose Paul in Acts 9, tell your spouse, "I chose you, and I still do."

8. An advantage adoptive parents have over biological parents is to say, "I chose you," a strong affirmation—*and* the child cannot boast in it, because the child was not the decisive chooser.

9. Write to children. An enthusiastic and thankful mother of some youngsters wrote me after I had first written her young sons, thanking them for their hospitality (God is very hospitable) in serving me a muffin when I visited their home for an interview related to child dedications at our church. To show the significance of my note (and stickers) sent to the boys, she quoted one of them as saying, "Tall men don't usually send you letters." It is hard to calculate the lasting effect of an affirmation given to a child.

10. Share a valuable secret of yours, making it known to the other person that very few others (if any) have been invited into this inner circle of those considered trustworthy.

11. Loan something of value—books, camping gear, a car, a cabin—as a signal of your willingness to take a risk, having noticed something in the other person that elevates your confidence in her trustworthiness.

12. Think of something that is normally not praised, because it is simply expected—like refilling the soap dispensers in the church restrooms. Customarily, those who have responsibilities for such things as refilling soap dispensers only hear from people when the dispensers are empty. Be the one to notice that they are *not* empty, and commend the faithfulness of the worker who serves others behind the scenes.

13. In the next birthday card or Christmas card you send, include a personal note commending some Christlike quality you observe in the recipient.

14. Compose a letter to the editor affirming a character quality being demonstrated in the community.

15. Commend someone for the (sensitivity, kindness, compassion, etc.) with which he treated a third party. You noticed, and so does God.

16. Quote someone positively in his presence. "I agree with Jacob here, who said . . ."

17. Shannon Archer, a mother of several young children in our church, affirms her own children by affirming *all* children who demonstrate certain character qualities, saying within earshot of her children, "I'm so pleased with children who put away their things (or speak kindly to their siblings, or . . .)" when she sees one of them behaving in that very way. Talking this way affirms the child in question, explicitly elevates the principle being taught and applied, and holds out hope to other children who might be eavesdropping that if they demonstrate the same kind of character, they too will please mommy.

18. Get up from your chair, go to another room, seek out a person, and simply say something like, "I just came to say 'hi' (or 'good morning,' or 'have a great day,' or 'I appreciate you for . . .')." Admittedly, in some relationships that may seem forced, but it will generally be welcomed as a light-hearted affirmation of a person's existence.

19. Say, "I thank God for you."

20. When asked to do a chore, consider saying something like, "Nothing would give me more pleasure right now than doing this for you," because of all the tasks in the universe you could be doing, you choose to do this one. Serving someone can be affirming of them.

21. Nominate someone for an office or post—based upon her integrity, dependability, or trustworthiness.

22. Following a worship service, write a note or leave a voice mail for someone who excelled in reverential musicality, hospitable ushering, enthusiastic reading, or faithful preaching.

23. Meditate on how God affirms his Son in such places as Matthew 17:5 and Hebrews 1:5–9. Ask him to help you be that way toward your own sons, etc.

24. Take a family member to your closet and ask him to pick out what you should wear the next day, affirming his choices.

25. Show a child a place in your yard where you intend to plant flowers. Take him with you to the garden shop to select the plants.

26. Invite a small child to assist you in baking something by handling the ingredients and contributing decisions along the way (the red sprinkles or the blue?).

27. At a family gathering, invite everyone to mention something they admire about (Cousin Siegfried, or Aunt Rosie, or Mom, or . . .).

28. Tell someone you were praying for him and wanted him to know that God placed him on your heart.

29. When walking past someone, simply touch him in an appropriate way—a small pat on the back, a friendly nudge with elbow, etc.

30. Respond to that e-mail or note that has been waiting for a response.

31. Complete that task, chore, or request that your spouse asked you to do. It shows you value him or her by listening and acting.

32. When in an argument with your spouse or other family members, take written notes so that you can accurately

reflect back to them what you are hearing (affirming the importance of what they are saying) and can take away to-dos.

33. Post the creative work of children, commenting on some aspect of character that was demonstrated in the work—attention to detail, creative use of materials, generosity in sharing the work, etc.

34. Teach a youngster to drive.

35. When a staff member has invested extra time at work, send a note to the *spouse*, perhaps with flowers or a gift card, expressing appreciation for the generosity in sharing the husband or wife.

36. Ask someone's advice.

37. Ask a younger person's advice.

38. Take that advice. Act on it.

39. Paul said to the Corinthians, "Be imitators of me, as I am of Christ" (1 Cor. 11:1). Say to someone, "You are like Christ in (forbearance, boldness, etc.), and I want to imitate you as you imitate Christ."

40. Resolve that before you do any other work at the office or shop or school today, you will affirm a coworker or fellow student.

41. If you see yourself as not especially articulate toward your spouse, stand in front of an anniversary card rack and study some of the phrases used. Then write your own card.

I need to do this!!

42. Jesus is never late. His timing is perfect. While waiting for the start of a meeting, commend those who were on time for their punctuality, which shows respect for the time of others.

43. Jesus is very alert and thorough. When someone brings a mistake or oversight to your attention, humbly acknowl-

edge your error and commend him for his alertness and thoroughness in catching it.

44. There's no one more dependable than Jesus. When someone completes a task you asked her to do, commend her dependability. Reliable people are a valuable asset. Take a moment to say so.

45. Stop and pray right now, asking God to help you to be affirming.

46. Stop again, and ask God to help you help *others* to enjoy being more affirming.

47. Do you know people who are suffering from an illness? They may be encouraged if you commend their endurance, patience, and determination (to stick with the therapy, etc.).

48. When around someone who is biting his tongue, commend that self-control, which is a powerful work of God in him.

49. Do you know of a missionary or someone else doing something risky but right? Commend the courage.

50. No one is more deferential to the Father than Jesus. Commend appropriate deference and a surrendered will when you see them.

51. When you read a biography and come across an incident or episode modeling great character, read it to someone or send a photocopy of the paragraph or page, saying something like, "This reminds me of you."

52. Write a Bible verse such as Hebrews 12:1 on a note card to someone, adding, "I think you do better at this than I do."

53. When someone spots a way to save money, commend his thriftiness.

54. Compare someone you know with a Bible hero.

55. Don't forget to say thank you to those who directly (or indirectly) benefit you.

56. When people enlighten you, inform you, or help you change your mind about something, commend them for their persuasiveness.

57. Think of the most humble person you know. Now praise that person's humility to somebody else who knows him.

58. When a child brings up something he heard in a sermon or in a class, praise him for his attentiveness.

59. When someone solves a problem without waiting to be asked, commend his initiative.

60. Commend a self-sacrificing mother for her loyalty to her children's welfare.

61. Draw favorable attention to the orderliness of someone's cubicle, desktop, bedroom closet, kitchen counter, filing system, yard, car interior, etc.

62. Praise the reverential obedience of children. Repeat.

63. When someone comes up with a good idea or solution that was overlooked by others, commend his resourcefulness and creativity.

64. When someone models how to make do in the midst of disappointing circumstances, affirm the rare commodity of contentment and its beauty.

65. When someone advocates for the relief of the suffering of someone else, praise the compassion being demonstrated.

66. When an idea or proposal is slowed down by someone who is expressing misgivings, express appreciation for the cautiousness, even if you're not persuaded by his arguments.

67. Is someone working hard? Trumpet his diligence.

68. Is someone on stand-by? Commend the availability.

69. Did someone adjust his plans when asked to do so? Affirm the flexibility.

70. Do you observe or hear about someone gladly sharing what is hers with someone else? Hold up such generosity as a model to be imitated.

71. Is someone taking pains to avoid hurting someone else? Commend that gentleness.

72. Praise mercy and forgiveness when you see offenses dropped and blessing returned for cursing.

73. Ask a good friend, "How do you think my wife would like to be praised and affirmed?" Then do it.

74. Ask people you know to tell you about the nicest compliments they ever received. (A question like this might make for a very good group discussion.) See what you can learn from what they report. Act on what you learn.

75. Search the Scriptures for ways people commend others. Do likewise.

76. The reader who has read this far in the list has probably made two generalizations about all these suggestions for affirmation: notice and verbalize.

77. When interrupted by someone, set aside what you are doing, turn squarely toward her, give her eye contact, and pay attention.

78. Nominate someone for something like Alum of the Year, or Outstanding Graduate, or Citizen of the Month by highlighting character qualities as the basis for your nomination.

79. Write a eulogy for a great person who died. Send it to someone saying, "You remind me of this person."

80. Write a eulogy for a living person. Send it to him with thanks and appreciation for demonstrating the character he does.

81. When hearing about the conclusion of a difficult court case, write the judge a note commending his wisdom in the pursuit of justice.

82. When you observe (or hear about) a youngster doing his chores, praise his sense of responsibility as evidence that he is growing up.

83. When someone avoids foolishly lumping things together that don't belong together (not throwing the baby out with the bath water), commend his discernment and ability to make distinctions.

84. Do you see someone who is good at welcoming others, inviting them to share in activities, meals, lodging, etc.? Commend the hospitality.

85. When someone makes provision for the needs of someone who is of a different language, culture, race, age, etc., commend the sensitivity.

86. Before starting the agenda of a meeting, commend someone present for some commendable quality.

87. Put down this list, pick up the phone, and call your (spouse, teammate, coworker, child, parent, etc.) with an affirmation. The point: don't save it until later.

88. Thank whoever it is who restocks the paper in the copy machine at work, church, etc. Thank him for humility of unseen service and dependability.

89. Explore the dictionary for a good word to use about somebody. Use it.

90. Commend a worker (postal clerk, bank teller, McDonald's cashier, grocery store check-out guy, etc.) for smiling and being cheerful.

91. Invite the passenger in your car to set the cabin temperature, the sound system volume, or the radio dial.

I don't know about this one

92. Literally applaud someone for doing something commendable.

93. Invite others to join you in the applause.

94. Ask God to make you as (wise, kind, faithful, enthusiastic, etc.) as someone you know who excels at that quality. Then tell that person you are praying that way.

95. Insert a character quality into the well-known birthday jingle, like this: "Happy birthday to you. Happy birthday to you. Happy birthday dear dependable Debbie. Happy birthday to you."

96. Make an acrostic of a person's name, using a character quality for each letter. For example, Vicki:

    Virtuous
    Innovative in solving household problems
    Courageous confronter
    Kind to aging parents
    Industrious

97. Award a bonus or pay increase, or tip your delivery boy, stating the relevance of Christlike character to your action.

98. Ask members of your small group how they affirm Christlikeness in others, or ask for fresh ideas. Ask how *they* like to be commended.

we shoud do this!?

99. Tell your wife, mother, sister, or daughter how she reminds you of the noble woman in Proverbs 31.

100. Create your own suggestion and plug it in here as number 100. Then demonstrate it.

Decision Grid

When is an issue important enough to correct? The following grid provides a helpful matrix for deciding when to correct someone and when to just let it go.

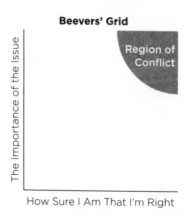

The vertical axis indicates the importance of the issue being considered. The bottom reflects issues of low importance such as trying to resolve whether President George Washington ever wore socks that didn't match. It is an issue of virtually no consequence. Moving up the axis, toward the top we reach issues that are important, issues that have life-and-death significance, perhaps for a great many people. Between the top and the bottom is an array of issues and their relative importance or unimportance.

The horizontal axis indicates my certainty that I am right. Toward the left are issues about which I don't have the foggiest clue (what is the name of the dog owned by the bit player in that 1938 movie that no one saw?). Toward the right are issues about which I am sure that I'm sure before God, the angels, and all the witnesses that could be summoned that I am right. Most people find that there are surprisingly few of these issues.

Any issue of controversy can be plotted on this matrix.

The lower-left quadrant contains issues that meet two simultaneous criteria: (1) they are of low importance, and (2) I do not know much about them. For example: how many angels can dance on the head of a pin? Who knows? And who cares? Here's the point: it wouldn't be worth consuming relational energy to argue about this issue or to correct someone else's viewpoint.

The upper-left quadrant contains issues that meet two simultaneous criteria: (1) they are of high importance, but (2) I still don't know with certainty what the truth is. For example: When is Jesus returning? That is of crucial and everlasting importance to every person who lives or ever *has* lived! And yet I don't know when he's coming back. One of the things about which I'm certain is that I am *not* certain about exactly when he's returning. The point is: arguing about it or correcting others is not worth the relational energy it would consume.

The lower-right quadrant contains issues about which (1) I'm certain I'm right, but (2) they are of low importance. For example: how many knots are in the log I am now looking at? I know the answer, but why make an issue of it?

And now we arrive at the main observation to be derived from Beever's Grid. The upper-right quadrant simultaneously contains the issues (1) that are important, and (2) for which there is virtually no possibility that I will be shown to be mistaken. And here's the point: reserve your conflict, your arguments, and your persistent corrections to that quadrant. Here's its corollary: keep that region small. The fruitfulness of correction tends to come from a smaller region than we assume. We default to making that region larger than is fruitful.

We wear people out by putting more issues in the upper-right quadrant than belong there.

*Beever's Grid copyright 1986 by Ernest Beevers. Used by permission.

Tone of Voice

Chapter 8 underscores the importance of tone of voice. I was asked by a mother of several children (and foster mother of several more) how to promote a more pleasant tone of voice around her busy home. With her permission, I share with you what I wrote to her.

Dear Deb,

Here are some tactics to employ in the overall strategy of training your children to be respectful, which is *more* than tone of voice, but *includes* tone of voice:

1. Model what you want from your children. If your own tone is exasperated while you try to get the children to speak sweetly, they will detect the hypocrisy, and your efforts will backfire.

2. Don't just point out bad speech—argumentativeness, sassiness, etc.—but commend *good* tone. And this is important: reward it. Reward it *immediately*. What's a reward? It may vary from child to child, but rewards can include hugs to exclamations of "good job!" to "Hey, everybody . . . did you hear that good tone of voice? Now that's what I want to be like when *I* grow up!" Make a game of it, and throw ten-second parties when something good happens.

3. At times *other* than when the tone is bad, talk about the value of good tone of voice. It wins friends. It builds confidence in the minds of others that they can trust you. It demonstrates maturity (read James 3:3–12). It sweetens the ambiance, the atmosphere, the environment; it makes you easier to be around.

4. There are times when it is the parent's job to be the referee, even the cop. So let me suggest that it is fair, just, wise, and loving to clarify the rules of the game, or the laws of the house. Perhaps like this: "My dear child, you say that you were not being argumentative or sassy, and so I will give you the benefit of the doubt on this one. But it is the last one. I am now telling you in advance that if you use that kind of speech again, the next time (not the second next time, but the *very* next time) I am going to consider it sassy, do you understand? That tone of voice in this family will be understood as sassy. And—listen to me now, look me in the eye and listen to me—if you use that tone of voice again, here is what I will do." And then name the consequence or punishment. Perhaps you will force them against their will to listen to Sam Crabtree sermon tapes, or something else awful. More seriously, if you haven't thought of an appropriate consequence, you might say something

like: "I'm not sure yet what I'll do if you use that tone of voice, but if I have to I will stay up nights thinking of some way to make you miserable for talking like that, because I love you, and I desire for you to grow into a wise, godly, Christlike adult, and that kind of speech is unacceptable, and it must be bridled."

> I hope this is hopeful and helpful.
> Sam

Acknowledgments

The Bible is remarkably absent of acknowledgments. Though the writers over and over give thanks to God, they do not mention their editors, wives, and mentors. One brief word of gratitude by Paul in Romans 16:4 is the only instance in the Bible I know where thanksgiving is possibly directed toward anyone other than God. Nevertheless, a book on affirmation without an acknowledgments page seems incongruous. To give thanks is no chore, but a happy pleasure for the grateful heart.

For years Vince and Kathy Johnson kept after me to write on this subject, an affirmation in and of itself. John Piper exhorted me to write, saying he "would be happy to be the tugboat to get it out of the harbor of your mind into the sea of the world." Justin Taylor, vice president of book publishing at Crossway, encouraged me to submit a manuscript.

Amanda Knoke, former editor for *Decision* magazine, and current director of communications at Bethlehem Baptist Church, donated hours of her personal time to dig through the initial chapters, lending very helpful counsel along the way. Tara Davis, editor, styled the content with her fine-toothed comb, making literally over a thousand improvements to this book, many small, but some big, and all of them helpful to the reader. Diane Fisher tracked down citation information for Beever's Grid.

Vicki Crabtree, wifely sounding board since 1973, continues to teach me about the importance of affirmation—and countless other things. How can I ever adequately express my thanks to God for you, Love?

The leaders and people of Bethlehem Baptist Church gave me a sabbatical to do something that would put wind in my sails. I wrote a book.

A parade of individuals through the years modeled risk-taking affirmation: Mr. Poff, who thought I could sing and play piano well enough as a third grader to risk having me perform for the Civic Club; Mr. Burke, who started a seventh grader on the eighth-grade basketball team; Art Kurtz, who hired a high-school kid to mow lawns and trusted me with his brand-new car, even after I struck a deer with it; Leigh Ann Luken, who hired a rookie schoolteacher; Marly Wilson, who nominated me for a statewide teaching award; Joe Colaw, who hired a rookie pastor; Keith Drury, who entrusted some writing projects to a relatively untested writer; John Piper, who hired me as his executive minister; and people who have written me personal notes of affirmation over the years, which are very significant. I still have them. What risk did they take? These people risked feeding my pride. Yes, affirmation is risky. Thanks for risking.

Notes

Foreword

1. C. S. Lewis, *Reflections on the Psalms* (London: G. Bles, 1958), 94.

Chapter 1: God-Centered Affirmation of Those Who Are Not God

1. Jon Bloom, executive director of Desiring God Ministries, letter to the Philippian Fellowship, June 2009.

2. Jesus also said very indicting things, describing his disciples as being of little faith and calling the Pharisees a brood of vipers and whitewashed tombs. I repeat: this book does not deny or forbid sober rebukes, chastisements, warnings, and correction, but that isn't its focus.

3. God is the gospel. See John Piper, *God Is the Gospel* (Wheaton, IL: Crossway, 2005).

4. I considered the exhortation "For God's Sake, Praise Somebody" as a heading for this section, but I ruled it out because of the double entendre, a crude impression. Meanwhile, its straightforward meaning is the truth at which we are aiming.

5. Piper, *God Is the Gospel*, 13.

Chapter 2: Key to Refreshing Relationships: The Simplicity

1. Applying 1 Corinthians 14:26 ("building up") and 2 Timothy 1:16–18 ("refreshed me") to the practice of affirmation might seem like a stretch. I realize that not all building up (e.g., corrective exhortation) is affirmation. And not all refreshment is affirmation (e.g., giving a cup of cold water). Strengthened faith is the aim of "building up" (Jude 1:20). However, one of the ways strengthened faith is manifested is in maturing Christlike character qualities. In affirming such qualities, they are more likely to be repeated, replicated, and further strengthened.

When Paul says, "I myself am satisfied about you, my brothers, that you yourselves are full of goodness, filled with all knowledge and able to instruct one another" (Rom. 15:14), his affirmation is explicit, and I suspect he is looking for even more such goodness in the Romans he is affirming.

2. Jesus warns us not to do good deeds in order to be seen by men (see Matthew 6), otherwise we lose our reward. If the purpose of affirming others is to show off what a wonderful person I am at affirming, I'm not as wonderful as I think. But providing refreshment for others and doing good things that are observed by others is not the same as doing those same things *in order* to be seen by them. The excellent wife described in Proverbs 31 has a *reputation* that comes from her works: "Give her of the fruit of her hands, and *let her works praise her in the gates*" (Prov. 31:31). Having her works result in praise is not the same as doing the works to show off, seeking praise from people. We should do our affirming out of amazement of God, who gives gifts to people and will reward us with mercy and with himself.

3. Is mercy earned? See chapter 6.

4. See The Lutheran Church Missouri Synod, "Encouragement for Busy Church Workers," http://www.lcms.org/ca/www/enews/Messagetext.asp?MsgId=4593/.

5. C. J. Mahaney, letter to author, May 15, 2009.

6. Alex Chediak Dot Com, "Affirmation Ratio: Husbands, Love Your Wives!" http://www.alexchediak.com/blog/2006/07/affirmation_ratio_husbands_lov.php/.

7. Thanks to Gretchen Held for this insight.

8. See appendix 2 for more on tone of voice.

9. Richard Baxter, *The Practical Works of Richard Baxter, Vol. 1: A Christian Directory* (Ligonier, PA: Soli Deo Gloria Publications, 1990), 203. Baxter is saying these things to warn against being flattered by unscrupulous types, but in making his warning he points to the principle to which I am pointing—namely, that people are influenced by those who commend them.

10. John Calvin, *Commentaries on the Epistles of Paul the Apostle to the Philippians, Colossians, and Thessalonians*, trans. and ed. J. Pringle (Grand Rapids: Baker, 2003), 172. The quote is from Calvin's commentary on Colossians 2:1, "For I want you to know. . . ." He writes, "He declares his affection towards them, that he may have more credit and authority; for we readily believe those whom we know to be desirous of our welfare."

11. See chapter 3 on God-centered affirmation, which shows that God's commendation of people is explicit in the Bible.

Chapter 3: Toward Greater Refreshment: The Complexity

1. A discussion of the "sandwich technique" can be found in Stephen Kohn and Vincent O'Connell's *6 Habits of Highly Effective Bosses* (Franklin Lakes, NJ: Career Press, 2005), which Marshall Loeb quotes in "The Art of the Critique," *MarketWatch*, August 7, 2007, http://www.marketwatch.com/story/theres-a-right-way-and-a-wrong-way-to-critique-employees/.

2. Gordon Cheng, *Encouragement: How Words Change Lives* (Kingsford, Australia: Matthias Media, 2006), 10.

3. Chuck Swindoll, letter to friends of Insight for Living, November 1986. Charles Schwab said, "I have yet to find the man, however exalted his station, who

did not do better work and put forth greater effort under a spirit of approval than a spirit of criticism." He also said, "I consider my ability to arouse enthusiasm among men the greatest asset I possess. The way to develop the best that is in a man is by appreciation and encouragement" (Charles Schwab, quoted in Woopidoo! Quotations, "Charles Schwab Quotes," http://www.woopidoo.com/business_quotes/authors/charles-schwab-quotes.htm). While some men have squandered their discovery (of the power of applause and approval) on temporal pursuits instead of eternal virtues, the power of affirmation that they commend remains valid, nonetheless. Just as secular award-winning writers have done a commendable job documenting the sinfulness of man without pointing to the Savior, and just as secular researchers have discovered cause-and-effect relationships in the worlds of physical and life sciences without pointing to the Creator, Schwab and others show us something of how God designed the universe of human relationships, even when they fail to point to the Lord of it all.

4. This quote is from a larger statement by Andy Stanley: "Every church celebrates something—attendance, membership, missions, new carpet—but often it's accidental rather than intentional. Whatever you celebrate reinforces a value in the minds and hearts of your people." Andy Stanley, "Building a Stewardship Culture in Your Church," Generous Steward, http://www.servethecity.org/pdf/LCAEBuildingAStewardshipCulture.pdf/.

Chapter 5: Mistakes I Have Made

1. John Piper, "Hero Worship and Holy Emulation," Desiring God, June 10, 2009, http://www.desiringgod.org/ResourceLibrary/TasteAndSee/ByDate/2009/3974_Hero_Worship_and_Holy_Emulation/.

2. A "propitiating substitute" is someone who takes the sinner's place, absorbing the wrath and punishment his sinfulness deserves. "Alien righteousness" is the guiltless record and proactive obedience of another party being credited to the sinner. Jesus is both propitiating substitute and alien righteousness for all who look away from their own self-justification to his advocacy for them.

3. I once coached a basketball team to an undefeated season, and while my memory might be playing tricks on me, I don't remember *ever* scolding the players, but I do remember lots of "Good job! Good thinking! Good hustle!" along with hours of instruction during which I corrected errors in performance by commending better ways of playing the game.

4. C. S. Lewis, *Mere Christianity* (New York: Simon & Schuster, 1952), 178.

5. Matthew Henry, *Matthew Henry's Commentary on the Whole Bible*, vol. 6, *Acts to Revelation* (Peabody, MA: Hendrickson, 1991), 375.

6. I get this from "Do nothing from rivalry or conceit, but in humility count others more significant [*huperecho*—"better than"] than yourselves" (Phil. 2:3).

7. Edmund Burke, *Burke, Select Works*, ed. Edward John Payne (Clark, NJ: Lawbook Exchange, 2005), 9: "When I see the spirit of liberty in action, I see a strong principle at work; and this, for a while, is all I can possibly know of it. The wild *gas*, the fixed air, is plainly broke loose: but we ought to suspend our judgment until the first effervescence is a little subsided, till the liquor is cleared, and until we see something deeper than the agitation of a troubled and frothy surface. I must

be tolerably sure, before I venture publicly to congratulate men upon a blessing, that they have really received one. *Flattery corrupts both the receiver and the giver;* and adulation is not of more service to the people than to kings. I should therefore suspend my congratulations on the new liberty of France, until I was informed how it had been combined with government; with public force; with the discipline of armies; with the collection of an effective and well-distributed revenue; with morality and religion. . . ."

8. Mary Beeke, *The Law of Kindness* (Grand Rapids, MI: Reformation Heritage Books, 2007), 170.

9. A book that seeks to foster God-centeredness will receive severe criticism for citing with approval sources that are not God-centered. But, as the old adage goes, even the blind squirrel occasionally finds a nut. To absolutely forbid the recognition of God-glorifying rays beaming from things that are not themselves consciously God-centered is to miss one of the points of this book. There is a common grace in all God creates. He has left his image even in unrepentant sinners, and occasionally those sinners make observations about truth without knowing its source.

Chapter 6: Questions and Answers

1. George Body, quoted in Mary Wilder Tileston, *Joy and Strength* (Minneapolis: World Wide Publications, 1929), 110.

2. *The Minneapolis Star Tribune* ran an article by that title: Kate McCarthy, "Are We "Good-job!"-ing Our Kids to Pieces?" *Star Tribune*, April 8, 2009.

3. Ibid.

4. I tremble when I think I may see something in Scripture that I then do not find confirmed in commentaries written by much better exegetes than I. So, if I have missed the mark in understanding Jesus about lamps and eyes and have misled the reader, you who can set me straight are welcome and invited to do so.

5. John Piper posed that question to a group of us at a prayer gathering in the Shalom House chapel, Pine River, MN, in January 2009.

6. Excerpt of a letter received from Brenda Zaney, Nov. 14, 2005.

7. Lewis Carroll, *Through the Looking Glass* (Chicago: Rand McNally, 1917), 99.

Chapter 7: Sightings of Jesus

1. Lou Priolo, *Pleasing People* (Phillipsburg, NJ: P&R Publishing, 2007), 175.

Chapter 8: Mixing Correction with Affirmation

1. Lloyd John Ogilvie, *The Greatest Counselor in the World* (Ann Arbor, MI: Servant Publications, 1994), 118.

2. Amanda Knoke, director of communications at Bethlehem Baptist Church, Minneapolis, in a conversation with author, summer 2009.

Chapter 9: 100 Affirmation Ideas for Those Who Feel Stuck

1. Frederick William Faber, quoted in Mary Wilder Tileston, *Joy and Strength* (Minneapolis: World Wide Publications, 1929), 118.

Scripture Index